PLASTIC CANVAS
Christmas Tidings™

Table of Contents

CHAPTER ONE
Santa and Rudolph

6   Merry Days

8   St. Nick Tissue Cover

10   Santa Mask

12   Santa Bottle Cover

14   Reindeer Doorstop

17   Noel Gift Bags

19   Santa's Snack

22   Reindeer Stocking

24   Reindeer Frame

26   Reindeer Treat Holder

28   Reindeer Napkin Ring

CHAPTER TWO
Colonial Charms

31   Pin Weaving Ornaments

34   Noel Sign

36   Patchwork Stocking

39   Christmas House

43   Home for Christmas

46   Ginger People Trivets

48   Christmas Candle

50   Antique Lamppost

52   Quick Baskets

54   Heavenly Trio

CHAPTER THREE
Jolly Holly

59   Christmas Kitten

63   Holly Accents

65   Christmas Joy Blocks

66   Music Button Covers

68   Candy Cane Container

71   Holiday Table Runner

73   Striped Tissue Cover

74   Mantel Runner

77   Christmas Place Mat

CHAPTER FOUR
Nutcracker Suite

30   Nutcracker Doorstop

32   Treat Holder

34   Toy Soldier

37   Napkin Ring

38   Stocking

90   Match Holder

92   Frame

94   Tote

96   Soldier Doorstop

99   Tissue Cover

CHAPTER FIVE
Frosty Friends

102   Card Guard

104   Heart Warmer

107   Tic-Tac Snowman

111   Belly Bumpers

115   Perky Penguin

118   Winter Welcome

122   Snowman Tissue Cover

124   Snowman Treat Basket

CHAPTER SIX
Elfin Magic

128   Elf Stocking

130   Christmas Ornaments

136   Star Coasters and Bowl

139   Elf Napkin Ring

140   Elf Frame

142   Elf Door Hanger

144   Star Frame

146   Christmas Money Tree

148   Elf Doorstop

151   Elf Treat Holder

153   Ready, Set, Stitch

156   Stitch Guide

158   Acknowledgments

160   Index

Product Development Director ANDY ASHLEY
Publishing Services Manager ANGE VAN ARMAN
Plastic Canvas Design Manager MARILYN SHELTON
Product Development Staff MICKIE AKINS
TONYA FLYNN
DARLA HASSELL
SANDRA MILLER MAXFIELD
ALICE MITCHELL
ELIZABETH ANN WHITE
Editor JUDY CROW
Assistant Editor KRIS KIRST
Associate Editors JAIMIE DAVENPORT
SHIRLEY PATRICK
Graphic Designer GLENDA CHAMBERLAIN
Photography Supervisor SCOTT CAMPBELL
Photographer ANDY J. BURNFIELD
Photo Stylist MARTHA COQUAT

Chief Executive Officer JOHN ROBINSON
Marketing Director SCOTT MOSS

Customer Service 1-800-449-0440 OR
CUSTOMER_SERVICE@
NEEDLECRAFTSHOP.com
Pattern Services (903) 636-5140

CREDITS

Sincerest thanks to all the designers,
manufacturers and other professionals
whose dedication has made this book possible.

Special thanks to
Quebecor Printing Book Group, Kingsport, Tennessee

Library of Congress Cataloging-in-Publication Data
ISBN: 1-57367-117-7
First Printing: 2001
Library of Congress Catalog Card Number: 2001130542
Published and Distributed by
The Needlecraft Shop, Big Sandy, Texas 75755
Printed in the United States of America.

Visit us at NeedlecraftShop.com

Dear Friends,

*Take time to remember the gifts you receive
as a child at Christmas time. For most of us
there is usually one that stands out. I rememb
when I was six years old, I saw a bicycle at th
local hardware store. It was bright pink and
had purple streamers hanging from the hand
bars. It was absolutely the most beautiful thin
I had ever seen. I wanted it so much that ever
night before I went to bed, I would pray for
Santa to bring me that bicycle.*

*That same year my grandparents traveled
from Texas to New Mexico to be with us durir
the holidays. On Christmas Eve we all gathere
around the tree and started opening presents.
My grandmother had made me a doll with
blonde hair, green eyes and a freckle on its
cheek that looked just like me. I was so excitee
about the doll that I completely forgot about t
bicycle. The next morning when I woke up, I
ran to the den to see if Santa had come. Sure
enough, there was the bicycle I had asked for.
Looking back, I treasured that doll much mor
than the bicycle. I think the reason was that
the doll was handmade especially for me. I
realize now the love and care that went into
making the doll.*

*Christmas Tidings is filled with wonderful
gift ideas that are easy and fast-to-finish. Son
can easily be personalized, while others can b
customized to fit anyone's home decor.*

*Experience the joy and excitement this yea
of giving a handmade gift. What better way t
show your love than by sharing your talents
with others in the form of handcrafted gifts.*

Judy

Judy Crow

CHAPTER ONE

Santa and Rudolph

Invite these Christmas characters into your home to celebrate the holidays with fun and frivolity. Stitch a project of Santa or Rudolph to create magical moments of the season that are sure to bring smiles to the faces of everyone who sees them.

Merry Days

Deck the walls in your holiday home.
Add something extra to your home decor this Christmas.

SIZE: 9½" square [24.1cm].

SKILL LEVEL: Easy

MATERIALS:
- One sheet of 7-mesh plastic canvas
- No. 5 Pearl Cotton (Coton Perlé) Art. 116 by DMC® or six-strand embroidery floss; for amounts see Color Key.
- Needloft® Yarn by Uniek, Inc. or worsted yarn; for amounts see Color Key.

CUTTING INSTRUCTIONS:
For Picture, cut one 63w x 63h-holes.

STITCHING INSTRUCTIONS:

: Using colors and stitches indicated, work
picture according to graph; fill in uncoded
areas using sail blue and continental stitch.
With burgundy, overcast edges.

: Using pearl cotton or three strands floss
n colors and embroidery stitches indicated,
mbroider detail on Picture as indicated on
raph.

: Hang or display as desired.

— *Designed by Michele Wilcox*

COLOR KEY: Merry Days

Pearl cotton or floss	DMC®	AMOUNT
Dk. Garnet	#814	5 yds. [4.6m]
Black	#310	4 yds. [3.7m]
Dk. Delft Blue	#798	1 yd. [0.9m]

Worsted-weight	Need-loft®	YARN AMOUNT
Sail Blue	#35	25 yds. [22.9m]
Eggshell	#39	15 yds. [13.7m]
Fern	#23	10 yds. [9.1m]
Burgundy	#03	5 yds. [4.6m]
Silver	#37	3 yds. [2.7m]
Black	#00	2 yds. [1.8m]
Forest	#29	2 yds. [1.8m]
Tangerine	#11	¹/₂ yd. [0.5m]

STITCH KEY:

- Backstitch/Straight
- French Knot

Picture
(63w x 63h-hole piece) Cut 1 & work.

St. Nick Tissue Cover

Capture the magic of Christmas by stitching
this whimsical tissue cover of the jolly ol' fellow himself.

SIZE: Snugly covers a boutique-style tissue box.

SKILL LEVEL: Average

MATERIALS:
- Two sheets of 7-mesh plastic canvas
- Craft glue or glue gun
- Worsted-weight or plastic canvas yarn; for amounts see Color Key.

CUTTING INSTRUCTIONS:

A: For Front, cut one according to graph.
B: For Back and Sides, cut three (one for Back and two for Sides) 31w x 36h-holes (no graph).
C: For Top, cut one according to graph.
D: For Mustache, cut one according to graph.
E: For Eyebrows #1 and #2, cut one each according to graphs.
F: For Holly Leaves, cut two according to graph.
G: For Berry, cut one according to graph.

STITCHING INSTRUCTIONS:

1: Using colors and stitches indicated, work A and C-C pieces according to graphs; work B pieces according to Back & Side Stitch Pattern Guide. Omitting attachment areas, with matching colors, overcast cutout edges of C and edges of A and D-G pieces.

2: Whipstitch A-C pieces together according to Tissue Cover Assembly Diagram. Glue Mustache, Eyebrows, Holly Leaves and Berry to Front as shown in photo.

—Designed by Christina Lau

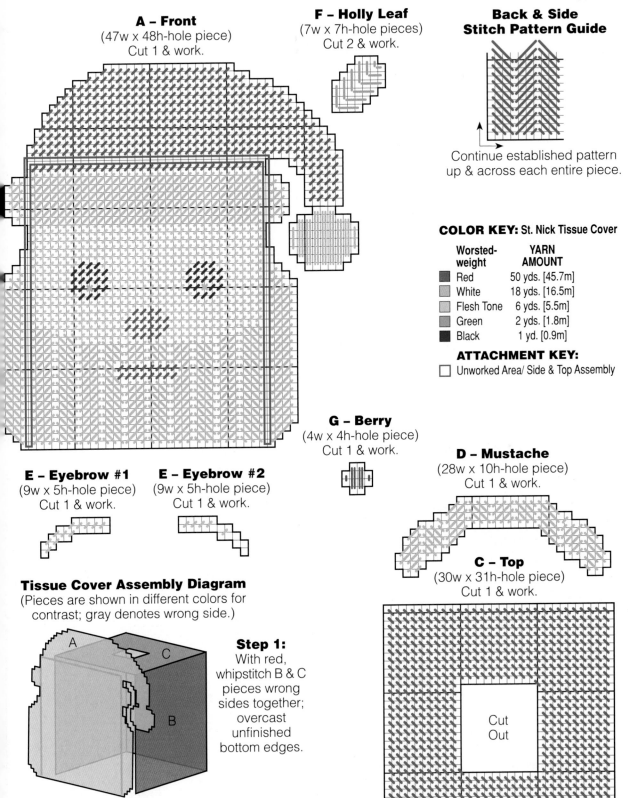

A – Front
(47w x 48h-hole piece)
Cut 1 & work.

F – Holly Leaf
(7w x 7h-hole pieces)
Cut 2 & work.

**Back & Side
Stitch Pattern Guide**

Continue established pattern
up & across each entire piece.

COLOR KEY: St. Nick Tissue Cover

Worsted-weight	YARN AMOUNT
Red	50 yds. [45.7m]
White	18 yds. [16.5m]
Flesh Tone	6 yds. [5.5m]
Green	2 yds. [1.8m]
Black	1 yd. [0.9m]

ATTACHMENT KEY:
☐ Unworked Area/ Side & Top Assembly

G – Berry
(4w x 4h-hole piece)
Cut 1 & work.

D – Mustache
(28w x 10h-hole piece)
Cut 1 & work.

E – Eyebrow #1
(9w x 5h-hole piece)
Cut 1 & work.

E – Eyebrow #2
(9w x 5h-hole piece)
Cut 1 & work.

C – Top
(30w x 31h-hole piece)
Cut 1 & work.

Tissue Cover Assembly Diagram
(Pieces are shown in different colors for
contrast; gray denotes wrong side.)

A
C
B

Step 1:
With red,
whipstitch B & C
pieces wrong
sides together;
overcast
unfinished
bottom edges.

Cut
Out

Step 2:
With white for beard areas & red for
hat area, whipstitch assembly to
unworked areas on wrong side of A.

Santa Mask

Keep your little one in smiles. Even Ebenezer Scrooge
himself would get a chuckle from this cheerful holiday mask.

SIZE: 6¼" x 20" [15.9cm x 50.8cm], including beard.

SKILL LEVEL: Average

MATERIALS:
• One sheet of 7-mesh QuickCount® plastic canvas
• Craft glue or glue gun
• Worsted-weight or Needloft® plastic canvas yarn by Uniek, Inc.; for amounts see Color Key.

CUTTING INSTRUCTIONS:
A: For Face, cut one according to graph.
B: For Mustache, cut one according to graph.

C: For Eyebrows #1 and #2, cut one each according to graphs.

STITCHING INSTRUCTIONS:
1: Using colors and stitches indicated, work pieces according to graphs. With flesh tone, overcast cutout and indicated edges of A; with white, overcast edges of B and C pieces.
NOTE: Cut forty-seven 1-yd. [0.9m] lengths of white.
2: For beard, attach one 1-yd. white length with a Lark's Head Knot to each ▲ hole on A as indicated; pull ends to even. Trim strands as desired to form beard.
NOTE: Cut one 18" [45.7cm] length of white.
3: For mask tie, thread one end of strand through each small cutout on side of Face; tie a slipknot in strand.
4: Glue Mustache and Eyebrows to Face as shown in photo. Use slipknot to adjust mask comfortably on head.

—Designed by Sandra Miller Maxfield

B – Mustache
(40w x 13h-hole piece)
Cut 1 & work.

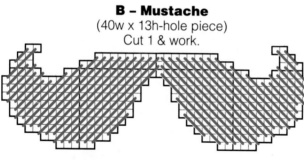

COLOR KEY: Santa Mask

Worsted-weight	Need-loft®	YARN AMOUNT
White	#41	60 yds. [54.9m]
Flesh Tone	#56	17 yds. [15.5m]
Pink	#07	4 yds. [3.7m]

STITCH KEY:
▲ Lark's Head Knot

C – Eyebrow #1
(11w x 6h-hole piece)
Cut 1 & work.

C – Eyebrow #2
(11w x 6h-hole piece)
Cut 1 & work.

A – Face
(41w x 30h-hole piece) Cut 1 & work.
Overcast between arrows.

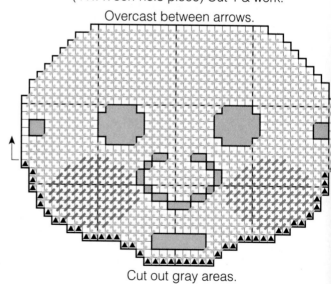

Cut out gray areas.

Santa Bottle Cover

Drink a toast of friendship,
old and new, with this jolly bottle cozy.

SIZE: Covers a 16.9 fl. oz. [500 ml] plastic soda bottle.

SKILL LEVEL: Average

MATERIALS:
- One Sheet of QuickCount® 7-mesh Plastic Canvas by Uniek, Inc.
- One 3" [7.6cm] QuickShape™ Plastic Canvas Radial Circle by Uniek, Inc.
- ½ yd. [0.5m] of green ⅝" [16mm] satin ribbon
- Craft glue or glue gun
- Worsted-weight or Needloft® plastic canvas yarn by Uniek, Inc.; for amounts see Color Key.

CUTTING INSTRUCTIONS:
A: For Side, cut one according to graph.
B: For Bottom, use circle (no graph).

STITCHING INSTRUCTIONS:
NOTE: B is not worked.
1: Using colors and stitches indicated, work A according to graph. Using black (Separate into individual plies, if desired.) and backstitch, embroider detail on A as indicated on graph.
2: Whipstitch and assemble pieces and ribbon as indicated and according to Bottle Cover Assembly Diagram.

— *Designed by Sandra Miller Maxfield*

COLOR KEY: Santa Bottle Cover

	Worsted-weight	Need-loft®	YARN AMOUNT
▨	White	#41	35 yds. [32m]
■	Red	#01	14 yds. [12.8m]
■	Baby Blue	#36	8 yds. [7.3m]
■	Black	#00	6 yds. [5.5m]
▨	Flesh Tone	#56	4 yds. [3.7m]
▨	Pink	#07	2 yds. [1.8m]
■	Bright Blue	#60	1 yd. [0.9m]
■	Royal	#32	1/4 yd. [0.2m]

STITCH KEY:
⊟ Backstitch

Bottle Cover Assembly Diagram
(Pieces are shown in different colors for contrast; gray denotes wrong side.)

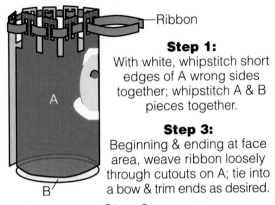

—Ribbon

Step 1:
With white, whipstitch short edges of A wrong sides together; whipstitch A & B pieces together.

Step 3:
Beginning & ending at face area, weave ribbon loosely through cutouts on A; tie into a bow & trim ends as desired.

Step 2:
Omitting cutouts, with red, overcast unfinished edges of A.

A – Side
(63w x 51h-hole piece) Cut 1 & work.

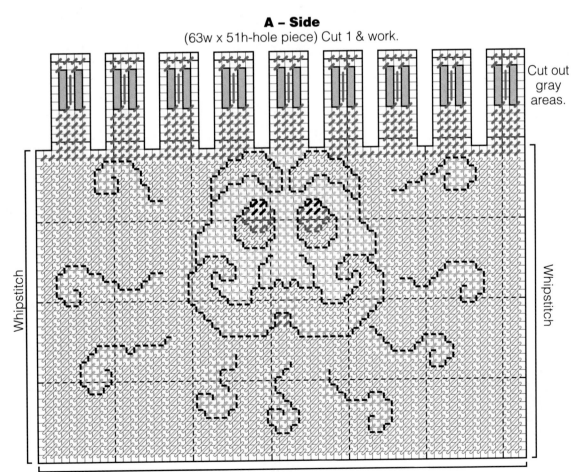

Cut out gray areas.

Whipstitch

Whipstitch

Whipstitch to B.

Reindeer Doorstop

Hold your door open for Santa and
his reindeer helpers with this cute holiday accent.

SIZE: 2½" x 14¼" x 10 ⅝" tall [6.4cm x 36.2 cm x 27cm].

SKILL LEVEL: Average

MATERIALS:
- Two Sheets of stiff clear 7-mesh QuickCount® Plastic Canvas by Uniek, Inc.
- Two 15mm oval wiggle eyes
- Thirteen gold 6mm beads
- 1 yd. [0.9m] natural raffia
- One zip-close sandwich bag filled with gravel or other weighting material
- Craft glue or glue gun
- Needloft® Craft Cord by Uniek, Inc.; for amount see Color Key.
- Needloft® Yarn by Uniek, Inc. or worste yarn; for amounts see Color Key.

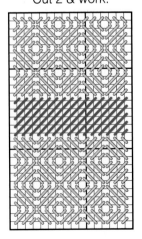

CUTTING INSTRUCTIONS:

A: For Back, cut one according to graph.
B: For Front, cut one 56w x 27h-holes.
C: For Top and Bottom, but one each [1]6w x 16h-holes.
D: For Sides, cut two 16w x 27h-holes.
E: For Tree, cut one according to graph.
F: For Reindeer Hooves, cut four [ac]cording to graph.
G: For Reindeer Nose, cut one according [t]o graph.

STITCHING INSTRUCTIONS:

[1]: Using colors and stitches indicated, work [A] (Leave ½" [13mm] loops on modified [t]urkey work stitches.) and B-G pieces [ac]cording to graphs. Omitting attachment [e]dges, with matching colors, overcast edges [o]f A and E-G pieces.
[2]: Using black (Separate into individual [p]lies, if desired.) and backstitch, embroider [m]outh on A as indicated on graph.
[3]: With matching colors, whipstitch B-D [p]ieces wrong sides together; whipstitch [a]ssembly to unworked area on right side of

A as indicated, inserting weighting material before closing.
4: Glue eyes, Nose and beads to Back as shown in photo. Glue one Hoof to each reindeer leg and to each Side as shown in photo.
NOTE: Cut raffia into six 6" [15.2cm] lengths.
5: Holding raffia lengths together, tie a knot in center; trim and fray ends as desired (see photo). Glue raffia knot to Front and Tree over raffia as shown.

—Designed by Kristine Loffredo

COLOR KEY: Reindeer Doorstop

	Metallic cord	Need-loft®	CORD AMOUNT
■	Red	#03	16 yds. [14.6m]

	Worsted-weight	Need-loft®	YARN AMOUNT
◪	Yellow	#57	30 yds. [27.4m]
■	Camel	#43	20 yds. [18.3m]
■	Christmas Green	#28	9 yds. [8.3m]
■	Black	#00	5 yds. [4.6m]
▨	Flesh Tone	#56	5 yds. [4.6m]
■	Brown	#15	2 yds. [1.8m]
■	Red	#01	1 yd. [0.9m]
■	Orchid	#44	½ yd. [0.5m]
■	Cinnamon	#14	¼ yd. [0.2m]

OTHER:
- ⊟ Backstitch/Straight
- ⊗ Modified Turkey Work
- ☐ Top & Side/Bottom Attachment

F – Reindeer Hoof
(9w x 7h-hole pieces)
Cut 4 & work.

G – Reindeer Nose
(5w x 4h-hole piece)
Cut 1 & work.

D – Side
(16w x 27h-hole pieces)
Cut 2 & work.

B – Front (56w x 27h-hole piece) Cut 1 & work.

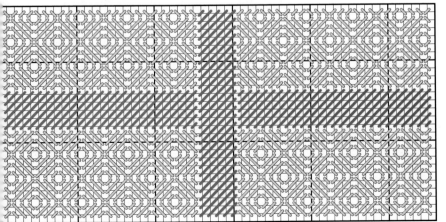

COLOR KEY: Reindeer Doorstop

Metallic cord	Need-loft®	CORD AMOUNT
Red	#03	16 yds. [14.6m]

Worsted-weight	Need-loft®	YARN AMOUNT
Yellow	#57	30 yds. [27.4m]
Camel	#43	20 yds. [18.3m]
Christmas Green	#28	9 yds. [8.3m]
Black	#00	5 yds. [4.6m]
Flesh Tone	#56	5 yds. [4.6m]
Brown	#15	2 yds. [1.8m]
Red	#01	1 yd. [0.9m]
Orchid	#44	1/2 yd. [0.5m]
Cinnamon	#14	1/4 yd. [0.2m]

OTHER:
- Backstitch/Straight
- Modified Turkey Work
- Top & Side/Bottom Attachment

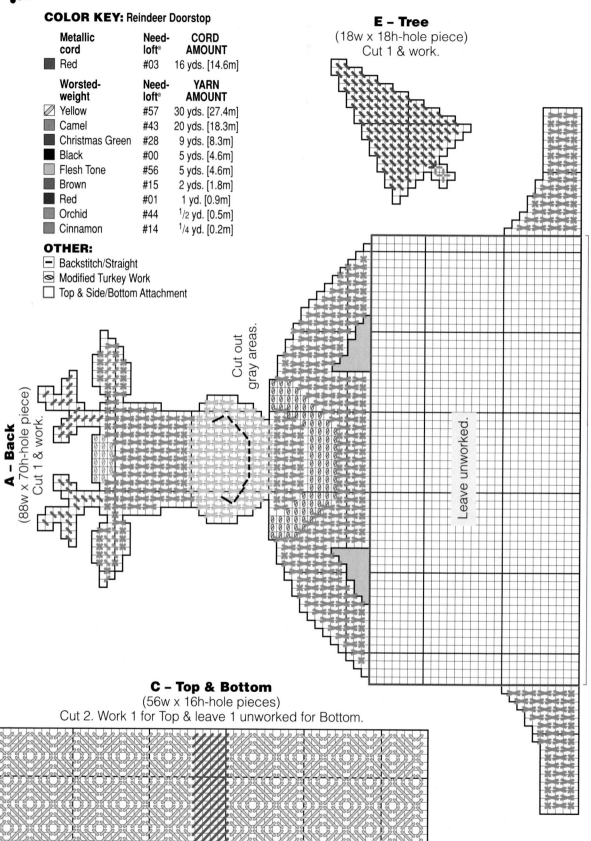

E – Tree
(18w x 18h-hole piece)
Cut 1 & work.

A – Back
(88w x 70h-hole piece)
Cut 1 & work.

Cut out gray areas.

Leave unworked.

Whipstitch to Bottom C.

C – Top & Bottom
(56w x 16h-hole pieces)
Cut 2. Work 1 for Top & leave 1 unworked for Bottom.

Noel Gift Bags

Package your best wishes along
with tiny treasures in these delightful treat bags.

SIZE: Each Bag is about 2½" x 4" x 5½" tall [6.4cm x 10.2cm x 14cm], not including Handle.

SKILL LEVEL: Average

MATERIALS:
- Two sheets of 7-mesh plastic canvas
- Six-strand Embroidery Floss Art. 117 by DMC®; for amounts see Color Key on page 18.
- Red Heart® Super Saver® Art. E300 by Coats & Clark or worsted yarn; for amounts see Color Key.

CUTTING INSTRUCTIONS:
NOTE: Graphs on pages 18 and 21.
A: For Tree Bag Front and Back, cut two (one for Front and one for Back) 25w x 36h-holes (no Back graph).
B: For Tree Bag Sides, cut two 16w x 36h-holes.
C: For Tree Bag Bottom, cut one 25w x 16h-holes (no graph).
D: For Tree Bag Handle, cut one 64w x 4h-holes (no graph).
E: For Santa Bag Front and Back, cut two (one for Front and one for Back) 25w x 36h-holes (no Back graph).
F: For Santa Bag Sides #1 and #2, cut one each 17w x 36h-holes (graphs on page 21).
G: For Santa Bag Bottom, cut one 25w x 17h-holes (no graph).

H: For Santa Bag Handle, cut one 65w x 4h-holes (no graph).

STITCHING INSTRUCTIONS:
NOTE: C and G pieces are not worked.
1: Using colors and stitches indicated, work one A for Front, B, one E for Front and F pieces according to graphs; work one A for Back, D, one E for Back and H pieces according to corresponding Stitch Pattern Guides. With grass green, overcast long edges of D; with cherry red, overcast long edges of H.
2: Using six strands floss in colors and

embroidery stitches indicated, embroider facial detail on Front E as indicated on graph.

3: For each Bag, with grass green for Santa and with matching colors for Tree, whipstitch corresponding Front, Back, Sides and Bottom together according to Bag Assembly Illustration on page 21; overcast unfinished top edges, catching short edges of corresponding Handle to Sides as indicated as you work.

—Designed by Phyllis Dobbs

COLOR KEY: Noel Gift Bags

Embroidery floss	DMC®	AMOUNT
■ Med. Brown	#433	1/4 yd. [0.2m]
▨ White	White	1/4 yd. [0.2m]

Worsted-weight	Red Heart®	YARN AMOUNT
■ Grass Green	#687	56 yds. [51.2m]
■ Cherry Red	#319	40 yds. [36.6m]
▨ White	#311	24 yds. [21.9m]
▨ Peach	#325	1 yd. [0.9m]
▨ Light Grey	#341	1/2 yd. [0.5m]
▨ Rose Pink	#372	1/4 yd. [0.2m]
■ Skipper Blue	#384	1/4 yd. [0.2m]

OTHER:
- ▬ Backstitch/Straight
- ● French Knot
- I Handle Attachment

Santa Bag Handle Stitch Pattern Guide
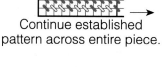
Continue established pattern across entire piece.

Tree Bag Handle Stitch Pattern Guide
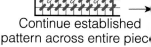
Continue established pattern across entire piece.

Tree Bag Back Stitch Pattern Guide
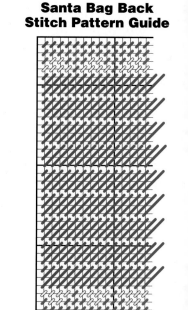
Continue established pattern across entire piece.

Santa Bag Back Stitch Pattern Guide
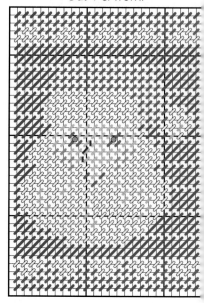
Continue established pattern across entire piece.

B – Tree Bag Side
(16w x 36h-hole pieces) Cut 2 & work.

Handle Attachment

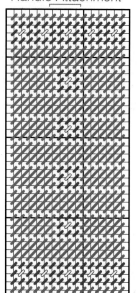

A – Tree Bag Front
(25w x 36h-hole piece) Cut 1 & work.

E – Santa Bag Front
(25w x 36h-hole piece) Cut 1 & work.

Santa's Snack

It's Kris Kringle at your service

when you treat guests to a favorite holiday beverage.

SIZE: 2" x 6½" x 6½" tall [5.1cm x 16.5cm x 16.5cm].

SKILL LEVEL: Average

MATERIALS:
- One sheet of 7-mesh plastic canvas
- One zip-close sandwich bag filled with gravel or other weighting material
- Craft glue or glue gun
- Six-strand embroidery floss; for amounts see Color Key on page 20.
- Worsted-weight or plastic canvas yarn; for amounts see Color Key.

CUTTING INSTRUCTIONS:

A: For Holder Back, cut one according to graph.

B: For Holder Front, cut one according to graph.

C: For Holder Bottom, cut one according to graph.

D: For Holder Side, cut one 11w x 7h-holes (no graph).

E: For Eyebrows #1 and #2, cut one each according to graphs.

F: For Cookies, cut four according to graph.

G: For Brace Front and Back, cut one each 10w x 17h-holes (no graph).

H: For Brace Sides, cut two 5w x 17h-holes (no graph).

I: For Brace Top and Bottom, cut one each 10w x 5h-holes (no graph).

STITCHING INSTRUCTIONS:

NOTE: G-I pieces are not worked.

1: Using colors and stitches indicated, work A, B (Leave ½" [13mm] loops on modified turkey work stitches.), C, E and F pieces according to graphs; work D using red and continental stitch. Omitting attachment edges, with matching colors, overcast edges of A-C, E and F pieces.

2: Using yarn and six strands floss in colors and embroidery stitches indicated, embroider detail on A and F pieces as indicated on graphs.

3: Whipstitch and assemble A-D and G-I pieces as indicated and according to Holder Assembly Diagram.

4: Glue Eyebrows to Holder Back as shown in photo. Cut through loops on Holder Front; trim and fray ends to fluff (see photo).

—Designed by Debbie Tabor

B – Holder Front
(21w x 16h-hole piece)
Cut 1 & work.

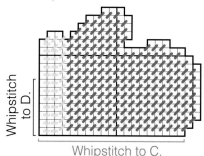

Whipstitch to D.

Whipstitch to C.

C – Holder Bottom
(31w x 6h-hole piece) Cut 1 & work.

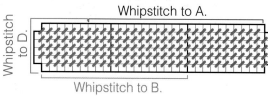

Whipstitch to A.

Whipstitch to D.

Whipstitch to B.

COLOR KEY: Santa's Snack

Embroidery floss	AMOUNT
Black	4 yds. [3.7m]
Blue	1 yd. [0.9m]
White	¼ yd. [0.2m]

Worsted-weight or plastic canvas yarn	YARN AMOUNT
White	16 yds. [14.6m]
Light Brown	12 yds. [11m]
Red	10 yds. [9.1m]
Flesh	7 yds. [6.4m]
Dark Brown	6 yds. [5.5m]
Turquoise	3 yds. [2.7m]
Black	2 yds. [1.8m]
Pink	1 yd. [0.9m]

STITCH KEY:
- Backstitch/Straight
- French Knot
- Modified Turkey Work

Holder Assembly Diagram
(Pieces are shown in different colors for contrast; gray denotes wrong side.)

Step 2:
With white, whipstitch A & C pieces together; glue opposite short end of D to wrong side of A.

Step 3:
For Brace, with red, whipstitch G-I pieces together, filling with weighting material before closing.

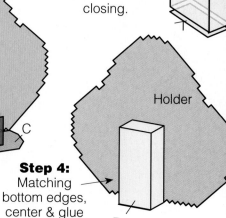

Step 1:
With white, whipstitch one short edge of D to B; with red, whipstitch B-D pieces together.

Step 4:
Matching bottom edges, center & glue Brace to wrong side of Holder.

A – Holder Back
(39w x 39h-hole piece)
Cut 1 & work.

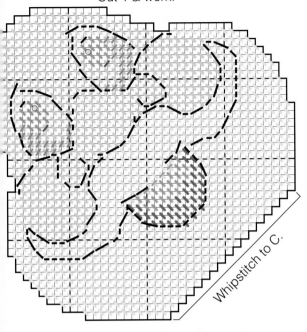

Whipstitch to C.

E – Eyebrow #1
(6w x 8h-hole piece)
Cut 1 & work.

E – Eyebrow #2
(6w x 8h-hole piece)
Cut 1 & work.

F – Cookie
(17w x 17h-hole pieces)
Cut 4 & work.

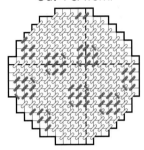

Noel Gift Bags

Instructions on pages 17 and 18.

– Santa Bag Side #1
(17w x 36h-hole piece)
Cut 1 & work.

Handle Attachment

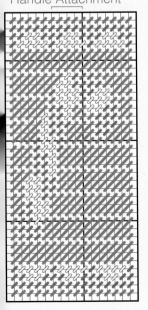

F – Santa Bag Side #2
(17w x 36h-hole piece)
Cut 1 & work.

Handle Attachment

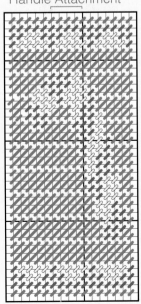

Bag Assembly Illustration
(Gray denotes wrong side.)

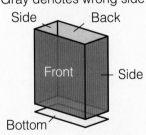

Side   Back

Front   Side

Bottom

COLOR KEY: Noel Gift Bags

Embroidery floss	DMC®	AMOUNT
Med. Brown	#433	1/4 yd. [0.2m]
White	White	1/4 yd. [0.2m]

Worsted-weight	Red Heart®	YARN AMOUNT
Grass Green	#687	56 yds. [51.2m]
Cherry Red	#319	40 yds. [36.6m]
White	#311	24 yds. [21.9m]
Peach	#325	1 yd. [0.9m]
Light Grey	#341	1/2 yd. [0.5m]
Rose Pink	#372	1/4 yd. [0.2m]
Skipper Blue	#384	1/4 yd. [0.2m]

OTHER:
- Backstitch/Straight
- French Knot
- Handle Attachment

Reindeer Stocking

Ready for Santa to fill,
this playful stocking is a gift in itself!

SIZE: 4½" x 13¼" [11.4cm x 33.7cm].

SKILL LEVEL: Average

MATERIALS:
• One Sheet of stiff clear QuickCount®

7-mesh Plastic Canvas by Uniek, Inc.
• One red ½" [13mm] pom-pom
• ½ yd. [0.5m] natural raffia
• Craft glue or glue gun
• Needloft® Craft Cord by Uniek, Inc.; for amount see Color Key.
  • Needloft® Yarn by Uniek, Inc. or worsted yarn; for amounts see Color Key.

CUTTING INSTRUCTIONS:
A: For Front, cut one accord ing to graph.
B: For Back, cut one accord ing to graph.
C: For Paws, cut two accord ing to graph.

STITCHING INSTRUCTION
1: Using colors and stitches indicated, work pieces according to graphs. Omittin attachment edges, with matching colors, overcast edges of pieces.
2: Using colors (Separate int individual plies, if desired.) and embroidery stitches indi cated, embroider detail on B and C pieces as indicated on graphs.
3: Holding A to matchir edges on right side of B, wi matching colors, whipstitc together as indicated. Glu pom-pom to Back and Paw to Front as shown. Tie raff into a bow and trim ends; glu bow to Front as shown.
—*Designed by Kristine Loffre*

A – Front
41w x 52h-hole piece) Cut 1 & work.

B – Back
(41w x 90h-hole piece)
Cut 1 & work.

Whipstitch to B
between arrows.

C – Paw
(6w x 6h-hole pieces)
Cut 2 & work.

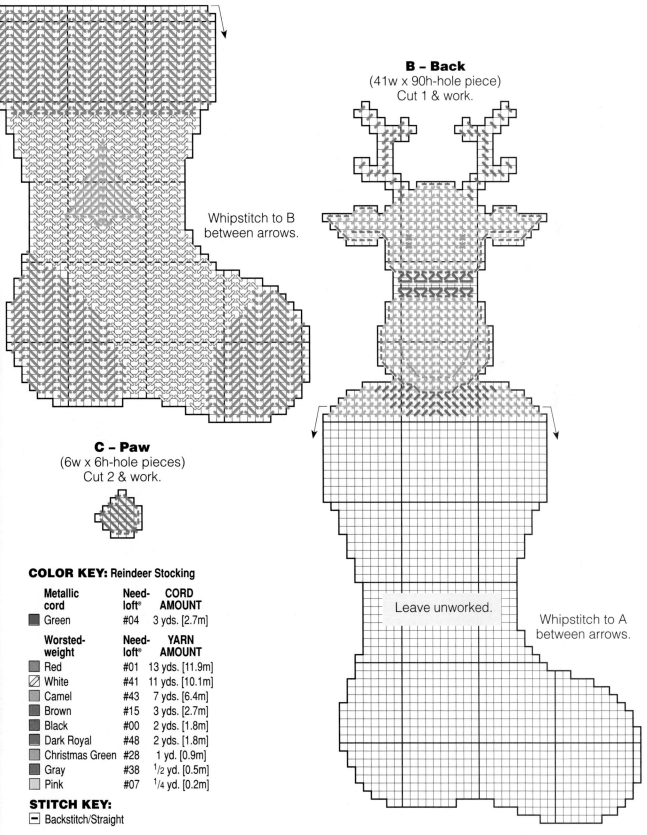

Leave unworked.

Whipstitch to A
between arrows.

COLOR KEY: Reindeer Stocking

Metallic cord	Need-loft®	CORD AMOUNT
■ Green	#04	3 yds. [2.7m]

Worsted-weight	Need-loft®	YARN AMOUNT
■ Red	#01	13 yds. [11.9m]
⊘ White	#41	11 yds. [10.1m]
■ Camel	#43	7 yds. [6.4m]
■ Brown	#15	3 yds. [2.7m]
■ Black	#00	2 yds. [1.8m]
■ Dark Royal	#48	2 yds. [1.8m]
■ Christmas Green	#28	1 yd. [0.9m]
■ Gray	#38	½ yd. [0.5m]
■ Pink	#07	¼ yd. [0.2m]

STITCH KEY:
- Backstitch/Straight

Reindeer Frame

Rudolph, with your nose so
bright! Capture the events of Christmas night.

SIZE: 4¾" x 6½" [12.1cm x 16.5cm] with a 3¼" x 5¼" [8.3cm x 13.3cm] photo window.

SKILL LEVEL: Average

MATERIALS:
- One Sheet of stiff clear QuickCount® 7-mesh Plastic Canvas by Uniek, Inc.
- Two 4mm wiggle eyes
- Four green holly leaf sequins
- Two red 8mm faceted beads
- Craft glue or glue gun

- Heavy (#32) and Medium (#16) Metallic Braids by Kreinik; for amounts see Color Key.
- Needloft® Yarn by Uniek, Inc. or worsted yarn; for amounts see Color Key.

CUTTING INSTRUCTIONS:
A: For Frame Front, cut one according to graph.
B: For Frame Back, cut one 41w x 28h-holes (no graph).
C: For Frame Stand, cut one according to graph.

D: For Reindeer Body, cut one according ⊃ graph.

E: For Reindeer Head, cut one according ⊃ graph.

TITCHING INSTRUCTIONS:

NOTE: B and C pieces are not worked.

1: Using colors and stitches indicated, work A (Omit stitches within attachment areas.) D and E (Leave ¼" [6mm] loops on modified turkey work stitches.) pieces according ⊃ graphs; with burgundy for Frame Front and with matching colors, overcast edges of A, D and E pieces.

2: Using yarn (Separate into individual

plies, if desired.), braid and cord in colors and embroidery stitches indicated, embroider detail on A, D and E pieces as indicated on graphs.

3: Whipstitch A-C pieces together as indicated and according to Frame Assembly Diagram. Glue eyes to E as indicated; glue Reindeer Head to Reindeer Body, forming Reindeer. Glue Reindeer, holly sequins and beads to Frame as shown or as desired.

—Designed by Kristine Loffredo

Frame Assembly Diagram
(Pieces are shown in different colors for contrast; gray denotes wrong side.)

Step 1:
With burgundy, whipstitch C to center of B at matching bottom edges.

Step 2:
Holding B to wrong side of A, work remaining stitches within attachment edges according to A graph.

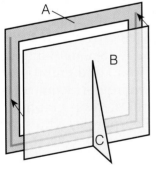

A – Frame Front
(43w x 30h-hole piece) Cut 1 & work.

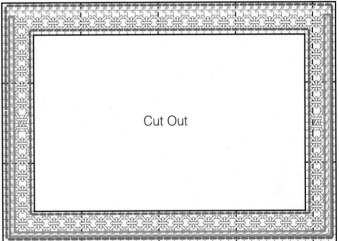

Cut Out

C – Stand
(8w x 24h-hole piece)
Cut 1 & leave unworked.

Whipstitch to B.

E – Reindeer Head
(13w x 20h-hole piece)
Cut 1 & work.

D – Reindeer Body
(9w x 20h-hole piece)
Cut 1 & work.

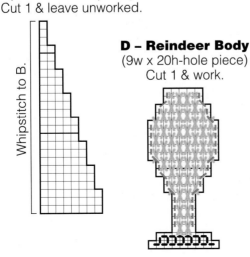

COLOR KEY: Reindeer Frame

Metallic cord	Needloft®	CORD AMOUNT
■ Green	#04	¼ yd. [0.2m]

Hvy. metallic braid	Kreinik	AMOUNT
■ Hibiscus	#326	4 yds. [3.7m]

Med. metallic braid	Kreinik	AMOUNT
■ Sapphire	#051C	3 yds. [2.7m]

Worsted-weight	Needloft®	YARN AMOUNT
▨ Flesh Tone	#56	10 yds. [9.1m]
▢ Burgundy	#03	8 yds. [7.3m]
▢ Camel	#43	5 yds. [4.6m]
▢ Cinnamon	#14	2 yds. [1.8m]
■ Black	#00	1 yd. [0.9m]
▨ Red	#01	¼ yd. [0.2m]

OTHER:
⊟ Backstitch/Straight
⊠ Modified Turkey Work
◯ Eye Placement
▢ Frame Front/Back Attachment

Reindeer Treat Holder

Reindeer party favors are sure to
delight your little elves as well as your sweet tooth.

SIZE: 2" x 6" x 7" tall [5.1cm x 15.2cm x 17.8cm].

SKILL LEVEL: Average

MATERIALS:
- One Sheet of stiff clear QuickCount® 7-mesh Plastic Canvas by Uniek, Inc.
- One red ½" [13mm] pom-pom
- Craft glue or glue gun
- Needloft® Yarn by Uniek, Inc. or worsted yarn; for amounts see Color Key.

CUTTING INSTRUCTIONS:
A: For Back, cut one according to graph.
B: For Front and Bottom, cut two (one for Front and one for Bottom) according to graph.
C: For Sides, cut two according to graph.
D: For Arms #1 and #2, cut one each according to graphs.
E: For Hooves, cut two according to graph.
F: For Holly, cut one according to graph.

STITCHING INSTRUCTIONS:
1: Using colors and stitches indicated, work A (Leave ½" [13mm] loops on modified turkey work stitches.), and B-F pieces according to graphs. Omitting attachment edges, with indicated and matching colors, overcast edges of A and D-F pieces.
2: Using colors (Separate into individual plies, if desired.) and embroidery stitches indicated, embroider detail on A, D and E pieces as indicated on graphs.
3: With bright purple, whipstitch Front B and C pieces wrong sides together and to right side of A as indicated. Whipstitch Bottom B to assembly; overcast unfinished edges of Front B and C pieces.
4: With camel, whipstitch D pieces to right side of A as indicated (see photo). Glue Arms to Sides and wrong side of one Hoof to each leg on right side of Back as shown in photo. Glue pom-pom to Back and Holly to Front as shown.

—Designed by Kristine Loffred

A – Back
(48w x 48h-hole piece)
Cut 1 & work.

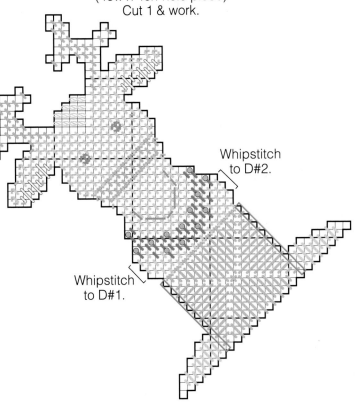

Whipstitch to D#2.

Whipstitch to D#1.

B – Front & Bottom
(18w x 18h-hole pieces)
Cut 2. Work 1 for Front & leave 1
unworked for Bottom.

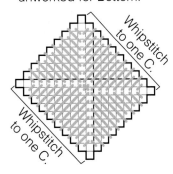

Whipstitch to one C.

Whipstitch to one C.

C – Side
(17w x 17h-hole pieces)
Cut 2 & work.

COLOR KEY: Reindeer Treat Holder

Worsted-weight	Needloft®	YARN AMOUNT
Bright Purple	#64	10 yds. [9.1m]
Camel	#43	8 yds. [7.3m]
Black	#00	5 yds. [4.6m]
Brown	#15	4 yds. [3.7m]
Christmas Green	#28	3 yds. [2.7m]
Christmas Red	#02	2 yds. [1.8m]
Forest	#29	2 yds. [1.8m]
Fern	#23	1 yd. [0.9m]
Flesh Tone	#56	½ yd. [0.5m]
Gray	#38	½ yd. [0.5m]

OTHER:
- Backstitch/Straight
- French Knot
- Modified Turkey Work
- Side/Back

D – Arm #1
(6w x 12h-hole piece)
Cut 1 & work.

Whipstitch to A.

D – Arm #2
(6w x 12h-hole piece)
Cut 1 & work.

Whipstitch to A.

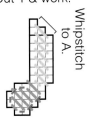

E – Hoof
(8w x 9h-hole pieces)
Cut 2. Work 1 & 1 reversed.

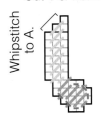

F – Holly
(9w x 5h-hole piece)
Cut 1 & work.

Overcast with Christmas red.

Reindeer Napkin Ring

Merry Christmas! Rescue your favorite
table from boredom with quick-and-perky napkin rings.

SIZE: 2" across x 4" tall [5.1cm x 10.2cm].

SKILL LEVEL: Average

MATERIALS:
- ½ Sheet of QuickCount® 7-mesh Plastic Canvas by Uniek, Inc.
- Craft glue or glue gun
- Medium (#16) Metallic Braid by Kreinik; for amount see Color Key.
- Needloft® Yarn by Uniek, Inc. or worsted yarn; for amounts see Color Key.

CUTTING INSTRUCTIONS:
A: For Napkin Band, cut one 44w x 4h-holes.
B: For Reindeer Body, cut one according to graph.

A – Napkin Band
(44w x 4h-hole piece) Cut 1 & work, overlapping ends & working through both thicknesses at overlap areas to join.

Lap Over   Lap Under

C: For Reindeer Head, cut one according to graph.

STITCHING INSTRUCTIONS:
1: Using colors and stitches indicated, work pieces (Leave ½" [13mm] loops on modified turkey work stitches.) according to graphs. With matching colors, overcast edges of pieces.
2: Using yarn (Separate into individual pli if desired.) and braid in colors and embroi dery stitches indicated, embroider detail or B and C pieces as indicated on graphs.
NOTE: Cut one 3" [7.6cm] length of Christmas green.
3: With ends at back, wrap green strand around Reindeer Head as shown in photo; glue ends at back to secure. Glue Reindeer Head to Reindeer Body as shown in photo; glue assembly to Napkin Band as shown.

—Designed by
Kristine Loffredo

C – Reindeer He
(11w x 17h-hole pie
Cut 1 & work.

B – Reindeer Body
(9w x 16h-hole piece)
Cut 1 & work.

COLOR KEY: Reindeer Napkin Ri

Med. metallic braid	Kreinik	AMOU
Sapphire	#051C	2 yds. [1

Worsted-weight	Need-loft®	YARI AMOU
Camel	#43	6 yds. [5
Christmas Green	#28	6 yds. [5
Cinnamon	#14	2 yds. [1
Black	#00	1 yd. [0
Red	#01	¼ yd. [0

STITCH KEY:
- Backstitch/Straight
- French Knot
- Modified Turkey Work

CHAPTER TWO

Colonial Charms

Decorate in true holiday style with accents
that radiate a subtle richness all their
own. These *Colonial Charms* are sure to
set a holiday mood in your home of
warmth and love as well as reflect the
joyous message of beauty, peace
and harmony.

Pin Weaving Ornaments

Trim your tree this Christmas with
special ornaments for your favorite time of year.

SIZE: Each is about 3" x 3½"
[7.6cm x 8.9cm].

SKILL LEVEL: Challenging

MATERIALS FOR ALL:
Two Sheets of 7-mesh Plastic Canvas
by Darice®
3" [7.6cm] length of metallic gold ⅛"
[3mm] chenille stem
⅛" [3mm] satin ribbon; for amounts
see Color Key.

CUTTING INSTRUCTIONS:
A: For Angel Front and Backing, cut two
(one for Front and one for Backing)
according to graph.
B: For Star Front and Backing, cut two
(one for Front and one for Backing)
according to graph.
C: For Stocking Front and Backing, cut two
(one for Front and one for Backing)
according to graph.
D: For Mitten Front and Backing, cut two
(one for Front and one for Backing)
according to graph.
E: For Snowman Front and Backing, cut
two (one for Front and one for Backing)
according to graph.
F: For Light Bulb Front and Backing, cut
two (one for Front and one for Backing)
according to graph.
G: For Tree Front and Backing, cut two
(one for Front and one for Backing)
according to graph.
H: For Heart Front and Backing, cut two
(one for Front and one for Backing)
according to graph.

STITCHING INSTRUCTIONS:
NOTES: Use ribbon lengths no longer than

18" [45.7cm]; longer lengths may split or
fray. For best results, keep ribbon flat
while stitching.
1: Using colors and stitches indicated, work
pieces according to graphs. For each
Ornament, holding Backing to wrong side
of matching Front, with desired ribbon
color(s) or color(s) shown in photo, whipstitch together.
2: For Angel's halo, twist ends of chenille
stem together, forming a halo; glue over
Angel's head as shown. Adorn and hang
ornaments as
desired.
—*Designed by*
Kathleen J. Fischer

COLOR KEY: Pin Weaving Ornaments

⅛" ribbon	AMOUNT
White	12 yds. [11m]
Green	10 yds. [9.1m]
Ivory	5 yds. [4.6m]
Mauve	5 yds. [4.6m]
Canary	4 yds. [3.7m]
Dk. Pink	3 yds. [2.7m]
Lt. Yellow	3 yds. [2.7m]
Red	3 yds. [2.7m]
Olive	2 yds. [1.8m]
Pink	2 yds. [1.8m]

B – Star Front & Backing
(20w x 23h-hole pieces)
Cut 1 & work according to Horizontal & Vertical Stitch
Pattern Guides (work vertical stitches first) for Front.
Cut 1 & leave unworked for Backing.

Vertical Stitch
Pattern Guide
(work first)

Horizontal Stitch
Pattern Guide
(Work last; see Weaving Illustration.)

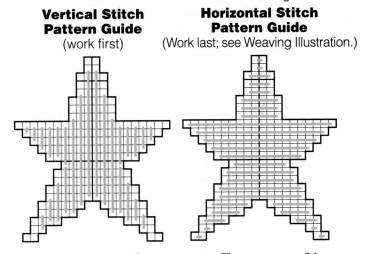

COLONIAL CHARMS

A – Angel Front & Backing
(24w x 23h-hole pieces)
Cut 1 & work according to Horizontal & Vertical Stitch
Pattern Guides (work vertical stitches first) for Front.
Cut 1 & leave unworked for Backing.

Vertical Stitch Pattern Guide
(work first)

Horizontal Stitch Pattern Guide
(Work last; see Weaving Illustration.)

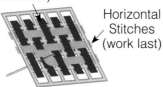

Weaving Illustration
(Ribbon colors shown in different colors for clarity.)

Vertical Stitches
(work first)

Horizontal Stitches
(work last)

D – Mitten Front & Backing
(21w x 23h-hole pieces)
Cut 1 & work according to Horizontal & Vertical Stitch
Pattern Guides (work vertical stitches first) for Front.
Cut 1 & leave unworked for Backing.

Vertical Stitch Pattern Guide
(work first)

Horizontal Stitch Pattern Guide
(Work last; see Weaving Illustration.)

COLOR KEY: Pin Weaving Ornaments

1/8" ribbon	AMOUNT
White	12 yds. [11m]
Green	10 yds. [9.1m]
Ivory	5 yds. [4.6m]
Mauve	5 yds. [4.6m]
Canary	4 yds. [3.7m]
Dk. Pink	3 yds. [2.7m]
Lt. Yellow	3 yds. [2.7m]
Red	3 yds. [2.7m]
Olive	2 yds. [1.8m]
Pink	2 yds. [1.8m]

C – Stocking Front & Backing
(20w x 23h-hole pieces)
Cut 1 & work according to Horizontal
Vertical Stitch Pattern Guides (work
vertical stitches first) for Front.
Cut 1 & leave unworked for Backing

Vertical Stitch Pattern Guide
(work first)

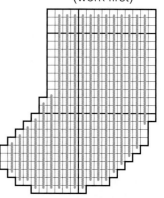

Horizontal Stitch Pattern Guide
(Work last; see Weaving Illustration.)

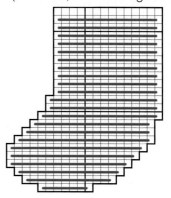

E – Snowman Front & Backing
(17w x 21h-hole pieces)
Cut 1 & work according to Horizontal & Vertical Stitch
Pattern Guides (work vertical stitches first) for Front.
Cut 1 & leave unworked for Backing.

**Vertical Stitch
Pattern Guide**
(work first)

**Horizontal Stitch
Pattern Guide**
(Work last; see Weaving Illustration.)

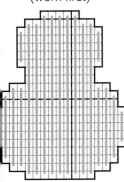
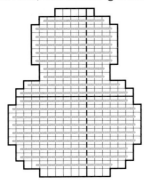

F – Light Bulb Front & Backing
(15w x 25h-hole pieces)
Cut 1 & work according to Horizontal & Vertical Stitch
Pattern Guides (work vertical stitches first) for Front.
Cut 1 & leave unworked for Backing.

**Vertical Stitch
Pattern Guide**
(work first)

**Horizontal Stitch
Pattern Guide**
(Work last; see Weaving Illustration.)

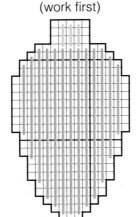
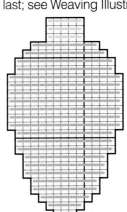

G – Tree Front & Backing
(21w x 23h-hole pieces)
Cut 1 & work according to Horizontal
& Vertical Stitch Pattern Guides (work
vertical stitches first) for Front.
Cut 1 & leave unworked for Backing.

**Vertical Stitch
Pattern Guide**
(work first)

**Horizontal Stitch
Pattern Guide**
(Work last; see
Weaving Illustration.)

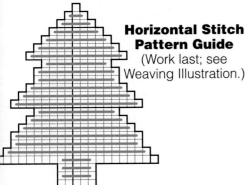

H – Heart Front & Backing
(21w x 20h-hole pieces)
Cut 1 & work according to Horizontal & Vertical Stitch
Pattern Guides (work vertical stitches first) for Front.
Cut 1 & leave unworked for Backing.

**Vertical Stitch
Pattern Guide**
(work first)

**Horizontal Stitch
Pattern Guide**
(Work last; see Weaving Illustration.)

Noel Sign

Add a special touch to your home decor this Christmas.

SIZE: 6¼" x 15½" [15.9cm x 39.4cm].

SKILL LEVEL: Average

MATERIALS:
- Two 12" x 18" [30.5cm x 45.7cm] or Larger Sheets of UltraStiff® 7-mesh Plastic Canvas by Darice®.
- ⅓ yd. [0.3m] red ¼" [6mm] satin ribbon

- Aleene's™ Designer Tacky glue or craft glue
- Needloft® Yarn by Uniek, Inc. or worsted yarn; for amounts see Color Key.

CUTTING INSTRUCTIONS:
A: For Sign Front and Backing, cut two (one for Front and one for Backing) 103w x 41h-holes (no Backing graph).

: For Wreath, cut one according
o graph.

TITCHING INSTRUCTIONS:

OTE: One A for Backing is
ot worked.

: Using colors indicated and conti-
ental stitch, work one A for Front
nd B pieces according to graph.
7ith Christmas green, overcast
dges of B.

: Using colors (Separate into indi-
idual plies, if desired.) and
mbroidery stitches indicated,
mbroider detail on Front A and B
ieces as indicated on graph.

: Holding Backing A to wrong
de of Front A, with Christmas
reen, whipstitch together. Glue
reath to Sign Front as shown in
hoto. Tie ribbon into a bow; glue
) Wreath as shown. Hang or dis-
lay as desired.

—*Designed by Jocelyn Sass*

COLOR KEY: Noel Sign

Worsted-weight	Need-loft®	YARN AMOUNT
☐ White	#41	51 yds. [46.6m]
■ Christmas Green	#28	15 yds. [13.7m]
■ Christmas Red	#02	8 yds. [7.3m]

STITCH KEY:
- ⊟ Straight
- ⊙ French Knot

B – Wreath
(16w x 16h-hole piece)
Cut 1 & work.

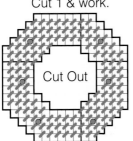

Cut Out

A – Sign Front
(103w x 41h-hole piece) Cut 1 & work.

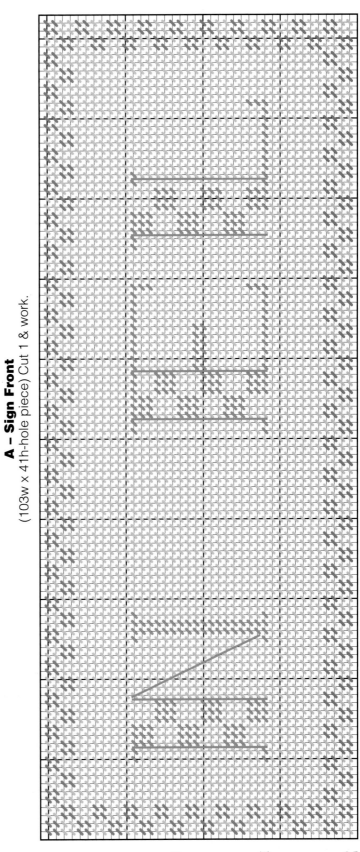

Patchwork Stocking

Bring old-fashioned Christmas charm
to your hearth with this patchwork stocking.

A – Side #1
(66w x 90h-hole piece) Cut 1 & work.

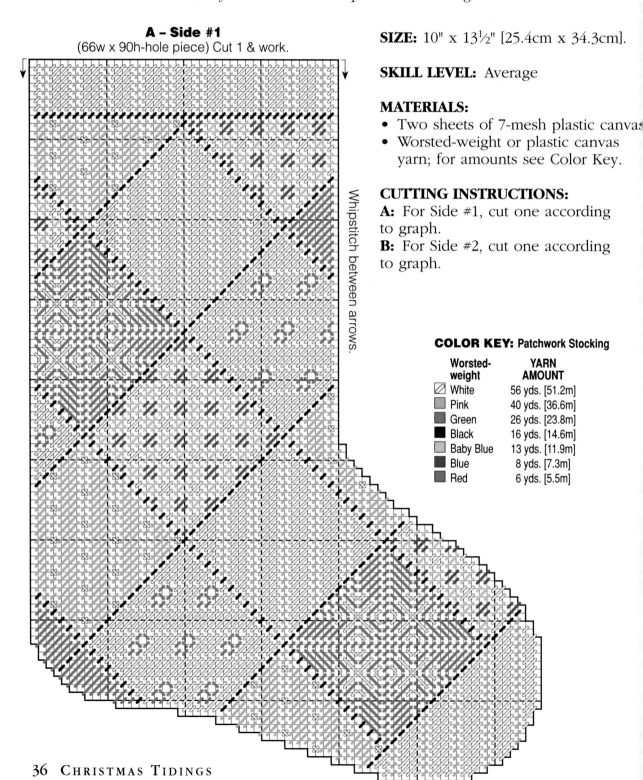

Whipstitch between arrows.

SIZE: 10" x 13½" [25.4cm x 34.3cm].

SKILL LEVEL: Average

MATERIALS:
- Two sheets of 7-mesh plastic canvas
- Worsted-weight or plastic canvas yarn; for amounts see Color Key.

CUTTING INSTRUCTIONS:
A: For Side #1, cut one according to graph.
B: For Side #2, cut one according to graph.

COLOR KEY: Patchwork Stocking

	Worsted-weight	YARN AMOUNT
⊘	White	56 yds. [51.2m]
	Pink	40 yds. [36.6m]
	Green	26 yds. [23.8m]
■	Black	16 yds. [14.6m]
	Baby Blue	13 yds. [11.9m]
	Blue	8 yds. [7.3m]
	Red	6 yds. [5.5m]

STITCHING INSTRUCTIONS:

1: Using colors and stitches indicated, work pieces according to graphs.

2: With matching colors as shown in photo, whipstitch pieces wrong sides together as indicated on graphs; with green, overcast unfinished top edges. Hang as desired.

—Designed by Alida Macor

COLOR KEY: Patchwork Stocking

	Worsted-weight	YARN AMOUNT
	White	56 yds. [51.2m]
	Pink	40 yds. [36.6m]
	Green	26 yds. [23.8m]
	Black	16 yds. [14.6m]
	Baby Blue	13 yds. [11.9m]
	Blue	8 yds. [7.3m]
	Red	6 yds. [5.5m]

B – Side #2
(66w x 90h-hole piece) Cut 1 & work.

Whipstitch to A between arrows.

Christmas House

Take care of those sniffles!
Top your tissues in North Pole style.

SIZE: Snugly covers a boutique-style tissue box.

SKILL LEVEL: Challenging

MATERIALS:
Two Sheets Each of White and Clear 7-mesh and One Sheet of Clear 10-mesh QuickCount® Plastic Canvas by Uniek, Inc.
One 7" [17.8cm] length of ¼" [6mm] wooden dowel
White craft paint and small paint brush
1¼ yds. [1.1m] red ⅛" [3mm] and ½ yd. [0.5m] red ¼" [6mm] satin ribbon
¼ yd. [0.2m] narrow green artificial garland with berries
Polyester fiberfill
Craft glue or glue gun
Six-strand embroidery floss; for amounts see Color Key on page 41.
Metallic yarn or cord; for amount see Color Key.
2-ply or sport-weight yarn; for amounts see Color Key.
Worsted-weight or plastic canvas yarn; for amounts see Color Key.

CUTTING INSTRUCTIONS:
NOTE: Use white 7-mesh for A-C pieces, 10-mesh for K-N pieces and clear 7-mesh canvas for remaining pieces.

A: For House Front, cut one according to graph.
B: For House Back, cut one according to graph.
C: For House Sides, cut two according to graph.
D: For Base, cut one according to graph.

E: For House Roof Pieces, cut two according to graph.

F: For Porch Roof Pieces, cut two from clear 7-mesh 18w x 6h-holes (no graph).

G: For Chimney Sides #1 and #2, cut two according to graph for #1 and two 14w x 11h-holes for #2.

H: For Large Shutters, cut six from clear 7-mesh 4w x 12h-holes (no graph).

I: For Medium Shutters, cut two from clear 7-mesh 2w x 12h-holes (no graph).

J: For Small Shutters, cut two according to graph.

K: For Wreath, cut one according to graph.

L: For Window Inset #1, cut one from 10-mesh 10w x 12h-holes.

M: For Window Inset #2, cut one from 10-mesh 16w x 25h-holes.

N: For Window Inset #3, cut three from 10-mesh 25w x 25h-holes.

STITCHING INSTRUCTIONS:

1: Using colors and stitches indicated, work A-E, G and J-N pieces according to graphs. Using dark green worsted and continental stitch, work F and I pieces; using dark green worsted and slanted gobelin stitch over narrow width, work H pieces.

2: With matching colors, overcast edges of D, F and H-K pieces. Using six strands floss, metallic yarn or cord and worsted yarn in colors and embroidery stitches indicated, embroider detail on A, G (omit stitches at seam edges) and K-N pieces as indicated on graphs.

3: Glue Window Inset #1 over small cutout and Window Inset #2 over large cutout on wrong side of House Front; glue one Window Inset #3 over cutout on wrong side of House Back and on wrong side of each House Side. With off-white, whipstitch A-C pieces wrong sides together, forming House; with matching colors, overcast unfinished top and bottom edges. Set assembly aside.

4: With dark green worsted, whipstitch E pieces wrong sides together as indicated; overcast unfinished edges. For Porch Roof,

whipstitch F pieces wrong sides together at one short end; overcast unfinished edges. With red worsted and alternating pieces, whipstitch G pieces wrong sides together as indicated; overcast unfinished edges. Using six strands black floss and backstitch, embroider remaining detail over seams of Chimney as indicated on G graphs. Set assemblies aside.

5: Glue Small Shutters near small cutout and Medium Shutters near large cutout on right side of House Front; glue two Large Shutters near cutout on right side of House Back and near cutout on right side of each House Side.

NOTE: Paint dowel and let dry; after dowel is dry, cut into two 3½" [8.9cm] lengths.

6: Wrap ¼" ribbon around each dowel length to form a candy cane effect, gluing ends to secure and trimming away excess as needed. Glue House over cutout on right side of Base; glue Porch Roof to House Front and dowels to Porch Roof and Base as shown in photo. Glue House Roof to House and Chimney to House Roof as shown.

NOTES: Cut ⅛" ribbon into five 9" [22.9cm] lengths; cut one 9" [22.9cm] length of metallic yarn or cord. Tie metallic yarn or

ord length and each ribbon length into a
ow; trim ends as desired.
: Glue metallic bow to Wreath and Wreath
 House door as shown. Glue artificial
arland under windows
round House, trimming
 achieve desired effect.
lue one red bow to
ach garland section as
hown. Glue fiberfill
round Base for snow.

—Designed by
Nancy Dorman

COLOR KEY: Christmas House

Embroidery floss	AMOUNT
■ Black	8 yds. [7.3m]
■ Red	8 yds. [7.3m]

Metallic yarn or cord	CORD AMOUNT
▨ Gold	8 yds. [7.3m]

Sport-weight	YARN AMOUNT
▨ Dark Green	20 yds. [18.3m]
▨ Pale Yellow	10 yds. [9.1m]

Worsted-weight	YARN AMOUNT
▨ Off-white	70 yds. [64m]
▨ Dark Green	60 yds. [54.9m]
▨ White	50 yds. [45.7m]
▨ Red	16 yds. [14.6m]

STITCH KEY:
- ⊟ Backstitch/Straight
- ⊡ French Knot
- ☑ Fly

A – House Front
(30w x 49h-hole piece)
Cut 1 from white 7-mesh & work.

Cut out gray
areas &
around bars
carefully.

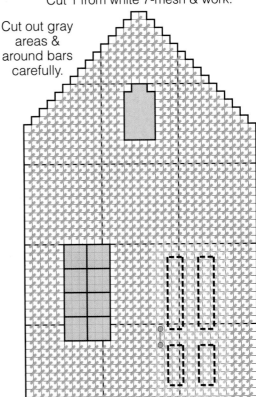

L – Window Inset #1
(10w x 12h-hole piece)
Cut 1 from 10-mesh & work.

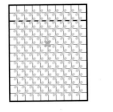

B – House Back
(30w x 49h-hole piece)
Cut 1 from white 7-mesh & work.

Cut out gray
areas &
around bars
carefully.

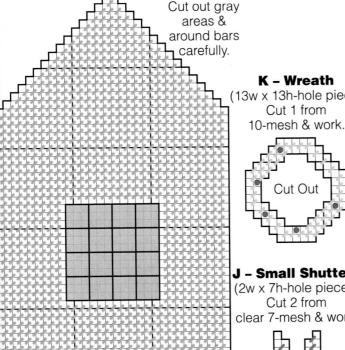

K – Wreath
(13w x 13h-hole piece)
Cut 1 from
10-mesh & work.

Cut Out

J – Small Shutters
(2w x 7h-hole pieces)
Cut 2 from
clear 7-mesh & work.

C – House Side
(32w x 35h-hole pieces) Cut 2 from
white 7-mesh & work.
Cut out gray areas & around bars carefully.

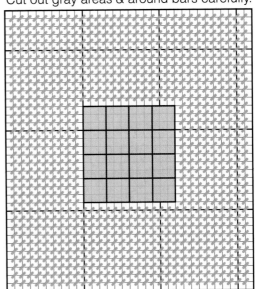

D – Base
(49w x 49h-hole piece) Cut 1 from clear 7-mesh & work.

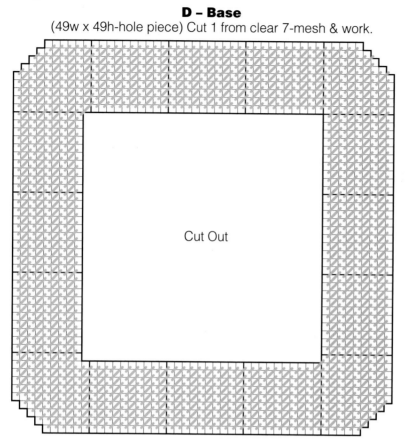

Cut Out

G – Chimney Side #1
(12w x 11h-hole pieces)
Cut 2 from clear 7-mesh & work

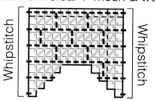

N – Window Inset #3
(25w x 25h-hole pieces)
Cut 3 from 10-mesh & work.

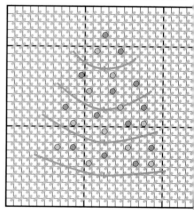

G – Chimney Side #2
(14w x 11h-hole pieces)
Cut 2 from clear 7-mesh & work.

COLOR KEY: Christmas House

Embroidery floss	AMOUNT
■ Black	8 yds. [7.3m]
■ Red	8 yds. [7.3m]

Metallic yarn or cord	CORD AMOUNT
■ Gold	8 yds. [7.3m]

Sport-weight	YARN AMOUNT
■ Dark Green	20 yds. [18.3m]
■ Pale Yellow	10 yds. [9.1m]

Worsted-weight	YARN AMOUNT
■ Off-white	70 yds. [64m]
■ Dark Green	60 yds. [54.9m]
■ White	50 yds. [45.7m]
■ Red	16 yds. [14.6m]

STITCH KEY:
- ⊟ Backstitch/Straight
- ⊙ French Knot
- ⋓ Fly

M – Window Inset #2
(16w x 25h-hole piece)
Cut 1 from 10-mesh & work.

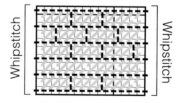

E – House Roof Piece
(37w x 29h-hole pieces)
Cut 2 from clear 7-mesh & work.

Whipstitch   Whipstitch

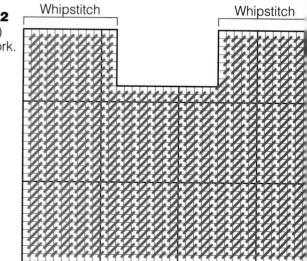

Home For Christmas

Holiday greetings to one and all.
Display your Christmas cards in a warm and cheery way.

SIZE: 7½" x 10½" [19cm x 26.7cm].

SKILL LEVEL: Challenging

MATERIALS:
- Two Sheets of Clear and ½ Sheet of Black QuickCount® 7-mesh Plastic Canvas by Uniek, Inc.
- One 14" [35.6cm] wooden ⅜" [10mm] dowel
- Two wooden 1¼" [3.2cm] knobs
- Americana® Alizarin Crimson DA179 Acrylic Paint by DecoArt™ and small paint brush
- 2½ yds. [2.3m] Green ⅝" [16mm] Satin Ribbon by Offray
- Ten ½"-across [13mm] round magnets
- Craft glue or glue gun
- Worsted-weight or Needloft® plastic canvas yarn by Uniek, Inc.; for amounts see Color Key.

CUTTING INSTRUCTIONS:
NOTE: Use black for F and clear canvas for remaining pieces.
A: For Banner, cut one 70w x 50h-holes.
B: For Banner Hangers, cut three 3w x 22h-holes (no graph).
C: For House, cut one according to graph.
D: For Snow, cut one according to graph.
E: For Large and Small Hearts, cut number indicated according to graphs.
F: For Letters, cut number indicated according to Letter Graph.

STITCHING INSTRUCTIONS:
1: Using colors and stitches indicated, work A and C-F pieces according to graphs. Using eggshell and reverse continental stitch, work B pieces. With matching colors, overcast edges of A-E pieces. (**NOTE:** F pieces are not overcast.)
NOTE: Separate black worsted into 2-ply or plastic canvas yarn into 1-ply strands.
2: With black, sew Small Heart to center right side of House as shown in photo. Holding Snow to House as indicated on C graph and House to center right side of

Banner (see photo), with black, sew together through all thicknesses.
NOTE: Paint dowel and knobs; let dry.
3: Sew Large Hearts and glue Letters to right side of Banner as shown or as desired. Glue one short end of each Banner Hanger evenly spaced across top edge of Banner (see photo); bend opposite ends and glue to back of Banner. Thread dowel through Hangers; glue one knob over each end of dowel (see photo).
NOTE: Cut seven 12" [30.5cm], one 9" [22.9cm] and two 6" [15.2cm] lengths of ribbon.
4: With longest lengths at outside edges (see photo), glue one end of two 12", 9" and 6" ribbons evenly spaced across bottom edge on wrong side of Banner (see photo). Tie each remaining 12" ribbon into a bow; glue one bow to opposite end of each ribbon length on Banner (see photo). Glue one magnet to back of each bow; attach one remaining magnet to secured magnet. Use magnets to temporarily hold cards on ribbon lengths.

—Designed by Sandra Miller Maxfield

E – Small Heart
(9w x 8h-hole piece)
Cut 1 from clear & work.

C – House
(28w x 23h-hole piece)
Cut 1 from clear & work.

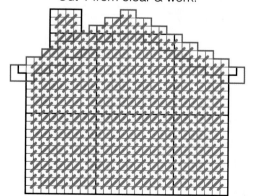

COLOR KEY: Home for Christmas

Worsted-weight	Need-loft®	YARN AMOUNT
Eggshell	#39	56 yds. [51.2m]
Red	#01	16 yds. [14.6m]
Royal	#32	8 yds. [7.3m]
Holly	#27	7 yds. [6.4m]
Black	#00	5 yds. [4.6m]
White	#41	4 yds. [3.7m]

OTHER:
- Backstitch/Straight
- Snow Placement

D – Snow
(30w x 9h-hole piece)
Cut 1 from clear & work.

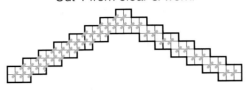

E – Large Heart
(11w x 10h-hole pieces)
Cut 2 from clear. Work 1;
substituting red for holly, work 1.

Letter Graph Cut 1 each from black & work.

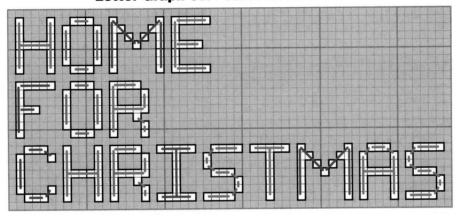

A – Banner (70w x 50h-hole piece) Cut 1 from clear & work.

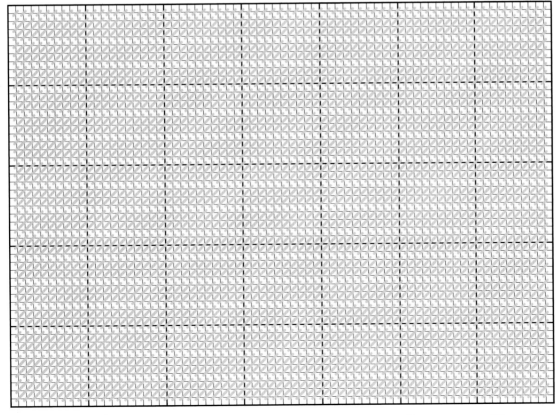

Ginger People Trivets

Warm your home with smiles
when you share homemade holiday treats.

SIZE: Girl is 6½" x 9" [16.5cm x 22.9cm]; Boy is 6½" x 8⅜" [16.5cm x 21.3cm].

SKILL LEVEL: Easy

MATERIALS:
• Two Sheets of QuickCount® 7-mesh Plastic Canvas by Uniek, Inc.

• Needloft® Craft Cord by Uniek, Inc.; for amount see Color Key.
• Needloft® Yarn by Uniek, Inc. or worsted yarn; for amounts see Color Key.

CUTTING INSTRUCTIONS:
A: For Girl Front and Backing, cut two (one for Front and one for Backing)

according to graph.
3: For Boy Front and Backing, cut two
(one for Front and one for Backing)
according to graph.

STITCHING INSTRUCTIONS:
1: Using colors and stitches indicated, work
pieces according to graphs. Using yarn
(Separate into individual plies, if desired.)
and cord in colors and embroidery stitches
indicated, embroider detail on Front A and
Front B pieces as indicated on graphs.
2: Holding Backing A to wrong side of
Front A, with white, whipstitch together;
holding Backing B to wrong side of Front
B, whipstitch together.

—Designed by Dawn Austin

B – Boy Front & Backing
(43w x 55h-hole pieces)
Cut 2.
Work 1 for Front
& leave 1 unworked for Backing.

A – Girl Front & Backing
(43w x 59h-hole pieces)
Cut 2.
Work 1 for Front & leave 1
unworked for Backing.

COLOR KEY: Ginger People Trivets

Metallic cord	Need-loft®	CORD AMOUNT
☐ Gold	#01	2 yds. [1.8m]

Worsted-weight	Need-loft®	YARN AMOUNT
☐ White	#41	40 yds. [36.6m]
☐ Maple	#13	30 yds. [27.4m]
☐ Holly	#27	11 yds. [10.1m]
☐ Christmas Red	#02	9 yds. [8.2m]
☐ Brown	#15	1 yd. [0.9m]

STITCH KEY:
⊟ Backstitch/Straight
⦿ French Knot

Christmas Candle

Light up those dreary winter
days with this festive holiday candle.

SIZE: 4⅞" across x 9" tall [12.4cm x 22.9cm], not including bulb.

SKILL LEVEL: Average

MATERIALS:
- One sheet of 7-mesh plastic canvas
- One of each 6" [15.2cm] and 4¼" [10.8cm] half-radial plastic canvas circle

- One standard 9" [22.9cm] electric candle with oval base
- Twenty-one 4mm pearls
- Two small artificial poinsettia leaves with greenery
- Craft glue or glue gun
- Worsted-weight or plastic canvas yarn; for amounts see Color Key.

CUTTING INSTRUCTIONS:
A: For Candle Side, cut one 47w x 48h-holes.
B: For Base Pieces #1 and #2, cut number indicated according to graphs.
C: For Base Bottom, cut away outer three rows of holes from 6" circle (no graph).
D: For Wax Top, cut one from 4¼" circle according to graph.
E: For Wax Side, cut one according to graph.

STITCHING INSTRUCTIONS:
NOTE: C is not worked.
1: Using colors and stitches indicated, work A, B, D and E pieces according to graphs. With red, overcast edges of A; with white, overcast cutout edges of D.
2: With white, whipstitch B pieces wrong sides together as indicated on graph; overcast unfinished top and notched edges of B pieces. Slide assembly over purchased candle, threading cord through notch on B#1; with green, whipstitch B and C pieces together, forming Base.
3: With white, whipstitch E to outer edges of D, forming Wax; overcast unfinished edges. Glue Wax over top of Candle Side (see photo). Screw bulb in purchased candle.
4: Glue pearls to Wax Side and poinsettias to Base as shown.

—Designed by Linda McGinnis

B – Base Piece #1

(12w x 13h-hole piece)
Cut 1 & work.

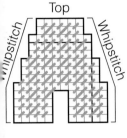

Top

Whipstitch   Whipstitch

B – Base Piece #2

(12w x 13h-hole pieces)
Cut 7 & work.

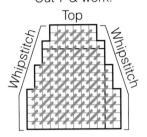

Top

Whipstitch   Whipstitch

D – Wax Top

(4 1/4" circle) Cut 1 & work.

Cut away
gray areas.

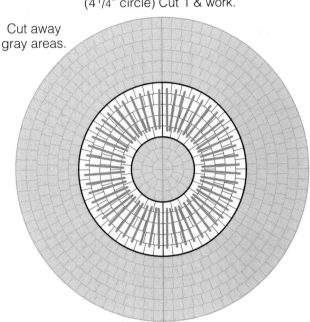

COLOR KEY: Christmas Candle

Worsted-weight	YARN AMOUNT
■ Red	35 yds. [32m]
▨ White	20 yds. [18.3m]
□ Green	2 yds. [1.8m]

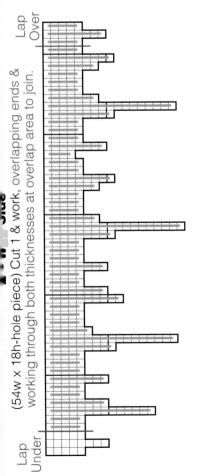

Lap Over

Lap Under

(54w x 18h-hole piece) Cut 1 & work, overlapping ends & working through both thicknesses at overlap area to join.

A – Candle Side

(47w x 48h-hole piece)
Cut 1 & work, overlapping ends & working
through both thicknesses at overlap area to join.

Lap Under

Lap Over

Antique Lamppost

Create a Charles Dickens
Christmas with this illuminating Antique Lamppost.

SIZE: 5" across x about 13" tall [12.7cm x 33cm], including finial.

MATERIALS:
- 2½ Sheets of QuickCount® 7-mesh Plastic Canvas by Uniek, Inc.

- One Welcome Candle Lamp by Darice® (bulb included)
- Beads by The Beadery:
    2 Gold 18mm Sunburst,
    1 Gold 12mm Sunburst
    1 Gold 10mm Round
    1 Gold 6mm Round
    Twelve red 8mm faceted beads
- 3" [7.6cm] red velvet bow
- Beading needle and clear sewing thread
- Fabri-Tac™ Fabric Glue by Beacon™ Chemical or craft glue
- Needloft® Cord by Uniek, Inc. or metallic cord (for amount see Color Key).
- Needloft® Yarn by Uniek, Inc. or worsted yarn (for amounts see Color Key).

CUTTING INSTRUCTIONS:
A: For Box Side, cut four according to graph.
B: For Box Bottom, cut one according to graph.
C: For Pole Side, cut four according to graph.
D: For Roof Side, cut four according to graph.
E: For Roof Top, cut one 10w x 10h-holes.
F: For Holly Leaves, cut four according to graph.

STITCHING INSTRUCTIONS:
1: Using colors and stitches indicated, work pieces according to graphs; with cord for Box Sides and black for Box Bottom, overcast cutout edges of A and B pieces. With holly, overcast edges of F pieces.
2: With beading needle and thread, sew round and sunburst beads together and to center right side of E according to Finial Assembly Illustration.

D – Roof Side
(32w x 18h-hole pieces)
Cut 4 & work.

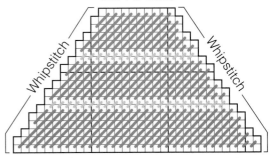

Whipstitch / Whipstitch

: Whipstitch and assemble A-E pieces as indi-
ated on graphs and according to Lantern
ssembly Diagram.
: Insert Welcome Candle base through bottom
pening of Lantern, then through cutout of
ox Bottom (see photo); secure bulb in base.
: Glue three facated beads to center of each
af (see photo); glue leaves to
p of Lamp.

—Designed by Carole Rodgers

F – Holly Leaves
(19w x 9h-hole pieces)
Cut 4 & work.

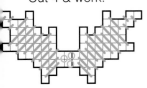

B – Box Bottom
(18w x 18h-hole piece)
Cut 1 & work.

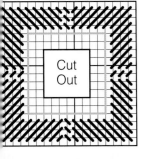

Cut Out

C – Pole Side
0w x 30h-hole pieces)
Cut 4 & work.

Whipstitch to B.

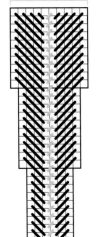

Finial Assembly Illustration
(Pieces are shown in different colors
for contrast.)

6mm
Round
Bead

12mm
Sunburst Bead

18mm
Sunburst
Bead

12mm
Round
Bead

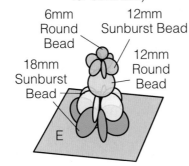

E

E – Roof Top
(10w x 10h-hole piece)
Cut 1 & work.

A – Box Side
(28w x 25h-hole pieces)
Cut 4 & work.

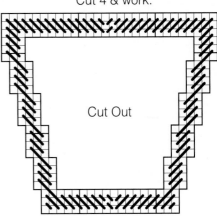

Cut Out

Lamp Assembly Diagram
(Pieces are shown in different colors for contrast;
gray denotes wrong side.)

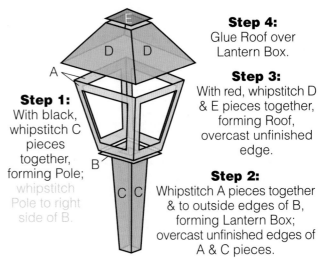

E
D   D
A
B
C C

COLOR KEY: Antique Lamppost

Metallic cord		AMOUNT
☐ White/Gold		12 yds. [11m]

Worsted-weight	Need-loft®	YARN AMOUNT
▦ Red	#01	42 yds. [38.4m]
■ Black	#00	30 yds. [27.4m]
▨ Holly	#27	8 yds. [7.3m]

ATTACHMENT:
☐ Pole
◯ Bead

Step 1:
With black,
whipstitch C
pieces
together,
forming Pole;
whipstitch
Pole to right
side of B.

Step 2:
Whipstitch A pieces together
& to outside edges of B,
forming Lantern Box;
overcast unfinished edges of
A & C pieces.

Step 3:
With red, whipstitch D
& E pieces together,
forming Roof,
overcast unfinished
edge.

Step 4:
Glue Roof over
Lantern Box.

Quick Baskets

Surprise a special friend with a sweet
treat presented in one of these yuletide baskets.

SKILL LEVEL: Challenging

MATERIALS:
- Two Green 5" [12.7cm] QuickShape™ Star Shapes by Uniek, Inc.
- Two Red 4" [10.2cm] QuickShape™ Radial Circles by Uniek, Inc.
- ½ sheet each green and red 7-mesh plastic canvas
- 8 yds. [7.3m] each red and green metallic cord or worsted-weight yarn (no Color Key).

CUTTING INSTRUCTIONS:
A: For Star Basket Sides, cut two from star shapes according to graph.
B: For Star Basket End/Bottom Piece, cut one from green 7-mesh according to graph.
C: For Heart Basket Side Pieces #1, cut four (two from each circle) from circles according to graph.
D: For Heart Basket Side Pieces #2, cut two from red 7-mesh according to graph.
E: For Heart Basket End/Bottom Piece, cut one from red 7-mesh according to graph.

STITCHING INSTRUCTIONS:
NOTE: Pieces are not worked.
1: For Star Basket, with green cord, whip-stitch A and B pieces together as indicated

SIZES: Star Basket is 2¼" x 5⅜" x 5¾" [5.7cm x 13.7cm x 14.6cm]; Heart Basket is 2¼" x 4⅜" x 4¾" [5.7cm x 11.1cm x 12.1cm].

B – Star Basket End/Bottom Piece
(68w x 14h-hole piece) Cut 1 from green 7-mesh & leave unworked.

Whipstitch to one A between arrows.

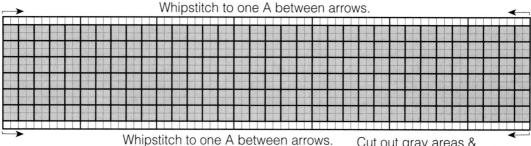

Whipstitch to one A between arrows.

Cut out gray areas & around bars carefully.

n graph. Wrap cord around remaining
dges of each Star to cover (see photo).
With red cord, whipstitch C-E pieces
ogether according to Heart Basket
ssembly Diagram.

—Designed by Debbie Tabor

Heart Basket Assembly Diagram
(Pieces are shown in different colors for contrast; cutouts not shown on E for clarity.)

Step 1:
For each Side (make 2), whipstitch two C & one D pieces together.

Step 2:
Whipstitch Side assemblies & E together; overcast unfinished outer edges of C pieces.

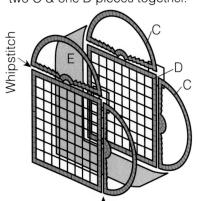

Whipstitch

C – Heart Basket Side Piece #1
(4" circle)
Cut apart 2 circles & leave unworked.

Cut out gray areas carefully.

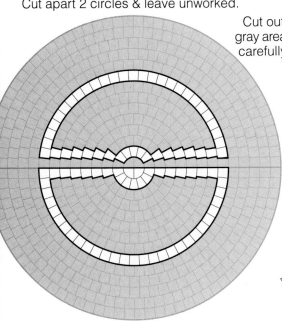

A – Star Basket Side
(5" star)
Cut 2 & leave unworked.

Cut out gray areas and around bars carefully.

Whipstitch to B between arrows.

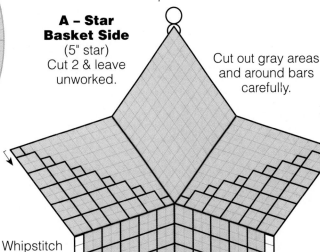

D – Heart Basket Side Piece #2
(20w x 20h-hole pieces)
Cut 2 from red 7-mesh & leave unworked.

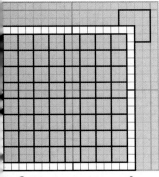

Cut out gray areas & around bars carefully.

E – Heart Basket End/Bottom Piece
(48w x 14h-hole piece) Cut 1 from red 7-mesh & leave unworked.

Whipstitch to one A between arrows.

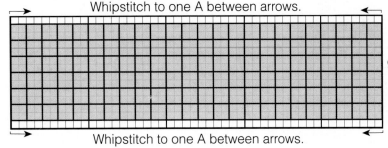

Cut out gray areas & around bars carefully.

Whipstitch to one A between arrows.

Heavenly Trio

Wing your way into a happier holiday
when you deck your home with this angelic trio.

SIZE: Each is about 5½" x 9½" [14cm x 24.1cm], not including hanger.

MATERIALS:

- 1½ Sheets of 7-mesh Plastic Canvas by Darice®
- Two 6" [15.2cm] QuickShape™ Plastic Canvas Hearts by Uniek, Inc.

- 2 yds. [1.8m] of 22-gauge wire
- Large curling iron or small piece of 1" [2.5cm] PVC pipe
- Craft glue or glue gun
- Metallic Cord (for amounts see Color Key)
- Needloft® Yarn by Uniek, Inc. or worsted yarn, (for amounts see Color Key).

CUTTING INSTRUCTIONS:

: For Skirts #1-#3, cut number indicated from heart shapes according to graphs.

: For Torsos #1-#3, cut one each according to graphs.

: For Shoes #1-#3, cut one each according to graphs.

: For Trumpets cut three according to graph.

: For Trees, cut nine according to graph.

: For Hearts, cut six according to graph.

STITCHING INSTRUCTIONS:

: Using colors and stitches indicated, work pieces according to graphs; with gold yarn for Trumpets and with matching colors, overcast edges of pieces.

: Using turquoise and backstitch, embroider detail on A#3 as indicated on graph.

: Glue wrong side of one Torso to right side of each corresponding Skirt as shown in photo; glue one Trumpet to wrong side of each Torso as shown.

NOTE: Cut wire into three 24" [61cm] lengths.

: For each hanger (make 3), wrap one wire around curling iron (do not heat) or pipe to coil; slip wire off curling iron or pipe. Glue three Trees and two Hearts to each hanger as shown; glue ends of hanger to wrong side of Skirt and Torso as shown.

—*Designed by Kristine Loffredo*

COLOR KEY: Heavenly Trio

Metallic cord		CORD AMOUNT
■ Turquoise		6 yds. [5.5m]
□ White		6 yds. [5.5m]
▨ Yellow Gold		2 yds. [1.8m]
▨ Solid Yellow		1 yd. [0.9m]

Worsted-weight	Need-loft®	YARN AMOUNT
▨ Bt. Blue	#60	30 yds. [27.4m]
■ Burgundy	#03	15 yds. [13.7m]
▨ Yellow	#57	12 yds. [11m]
■ Cinnamon	#14	10 yds. [9.1m]
▨ Beige	#40	6 yds. [5.5m]
■ Christmas Green	#28	5 yds. [4.6m]
▨ Christmas Red	#02	4 yds. [3.7m]
▨ Gold	#17	3 yds. [2.7m]
▨ Lavender	#05	3 yds. [2.7m]
■ Royal	#32	2 yds. [1.8m]

STITCH KEY:
- Backstitch/Straight

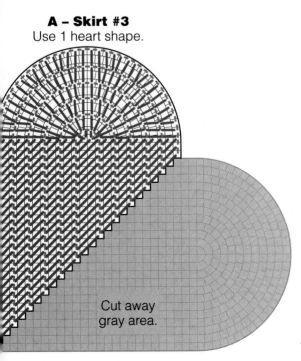

A – Skirt #3
Use 1 heart shape.

Cut away gray area.

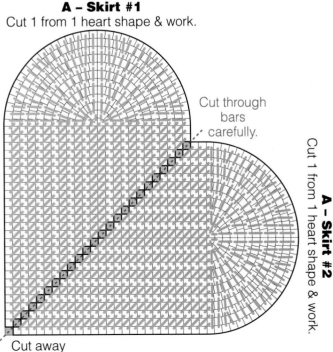

A – Skirt #1
Cut 1 from 1 heart shape & work.

Cut through bars carefully.

Cut away

A – Skirt #2
Cut 1 from 1 heart shape & work.

B – Torso #1
(45w x 21h-hole piece)
Cut 1 & work.

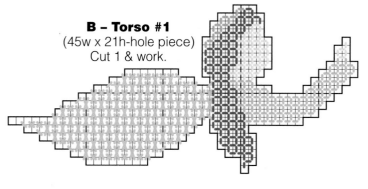

COLOR KEY: Heavenly Trio

Metallic cord		CORD AMOUNT
■ Turquoise		6 yds. [5.5m]
▫ White		6 yds. [5.5m]
▫ Yellow Gold		2 yds. [1.8m]
▫ Solid Yellow		1 yd. [0.9m]

Worsted-weight	Need-loft®	YARN AMOUNT
▫ Bt. Blue	#60	30 yds. [27.4m]
■ Burgundy	#03	15 yds. [13.7m]
▫ Yellow	#57	12 yds. [11m]
■ Cinnamon	#14	10 yds. [9.1m]
▫ Beige	#40	6 yds. [5.5m]
■ Christmas Green	#28	5 yds. [4.6m]
▫ Christmas Red	#02	4 yds. [3.7m]
▫ Gold	#17	3 yds. [2.7m]
▫ Lavender	#05	3 yds. [2.7m]
■ Royal	#32	2 yds. [1.8m]

STITCH KEY:
⊟ Backstitch/Straight

B – Torso #2
(45w x 21h-hole piece)
Cut 1 & work.

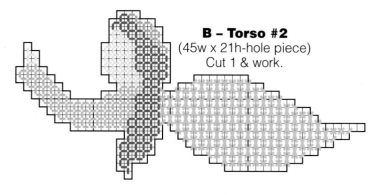

C – Shoe #1
(5w x 8h-hole piece)
Cut 1 & work.

C – Shoe #2
(5w x 8h-hole piece)
Cut 1 & work.

E – Tree
(6w x 6h-hole pieces)
Cut 9 & work.

C – Shoe #3
(5w x 8h-hole piece)
Cut 1 & work.

F – Heart
(5w x 5h-hole pieces)
Cut 6 & work.

D – Trumpet
(17 x 17h-hole pieces)
Cut 3 & work.

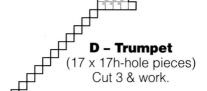

B – Torso #3
(46w x 23h-hole piece)
Cut 1 & work.

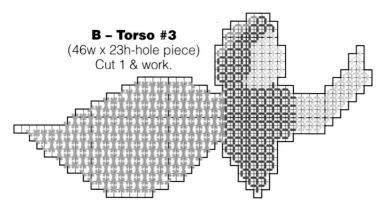

CHAPTER THREE
Jolly Holly

Add a touch of greenery here, a splash of holly berry red there as you deck the halls with boughs of holly. Fill each nook and cranny with the exciting magic of handstitched holiday decor by creating focal points throughout your home with these original decorating projects.

Christmas Kitten

This package-peeping Tom Cat
is sure to bring smiles to all.

SIZE: 1½" x 13½" x 22" [3.8cm x 34.3cm 55.9cm].

SKILL LEVEL: Average

MATERIALS:
Two 13½" x 22½" [34.3cm x 57.2cm] and Three Standard-size Sheets of QuickCount® 7-mesh Plastic Canvas by Uniek, Inc.
One white 1½" [3.8cm] pom-pom
Craft glue or glue gun
Worsted-weight or plastic canvas yarn; for amounts see Color Key.

CUTTING INSTRUCTIONS:
NOTE: Use large sheets for C and standard-size sheets for remaining pieces.
A: For Head Front and Backing, cut two (one for Front and one for Backing) according to graph.
B: For Paws, cut two according to graph.
C: For Package Front and Backing, cut two (one for Front and one for Backing) according to graph.
D: For Bow Loops, cut four according to graph.
E: For Bow Center, cut one 34w x 11h-holes.

STITCHING INSTRUCTIONS:
NOTE: One A and one C piece are not worked for backings.
1: Using colors and stitches indicated, work pieces according to graphs; fill in uncoded areas of Front A using sandstone and continental stitch. Omitting attachment edges, with matching colors, overcast edges of B, D and E pieces.
2: Using colors (Separate into individual plies, if desired.) and embroidery stitches indicated, embroider detail on Front A and B pieces as indicated on graphs.
3: For each Bow Loop (make 4), with dk. green, fold and whipstitch ends of one D wrong sides together as indicated. For Bow Center, fold and whipstitch ends of E wrong sides together as indicated.
4: Holding Backing A to wrong side of Front A, with matching colors, whipstitch together; repeat as above with B pieces.
5: Glue Head to back and paws to front of Package as shown in photo; glue pom-pom to tip of hat on Head as shown. Glue Bow Loops to center of Package front and Bow Center to Bow Loops (see photo). Hang or display as desired.

—*Designed by Candy Clayton*

COLOR KEY: Christmas Kitten

	Worsted-weight	YARN AMOUNT
	Dk. Green	2½ oz. [70.9g]
	Green	46 yds. [42.1m]
	White	40 yds. [36.6m]
	Sandstone	15 yds. [13.7m]
	Red	13 yds. [11.9m]
	Black	8 yds. [7.3m]
	Maple	6 yds. [5.5m]
	Camel	5 yds. [4.6m]
	Pink	5 yds. [4.6m]
☑	Eggshell	4 yds. [3.7m]
	Burgundy	1 yd. [0.9m]
☑	Watermelon	1 yd. [0.9m]

STITCH KEY:
- ▬ Straight
- ✳ Smyrna Cross

E – Bow Center
(34w x 11h-hole piece)
Cut 1 from standard sheet & work.

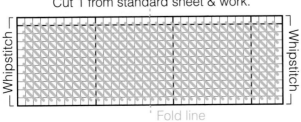

Whipstitch

Whipstitch

Fold line

JOLLY HOLLY

A – Head Front & Backing
(69w x 66h-hole pieces)
Cut 2 from standard sheets. Work 1 for Front & leave 1 unworked for Backing.

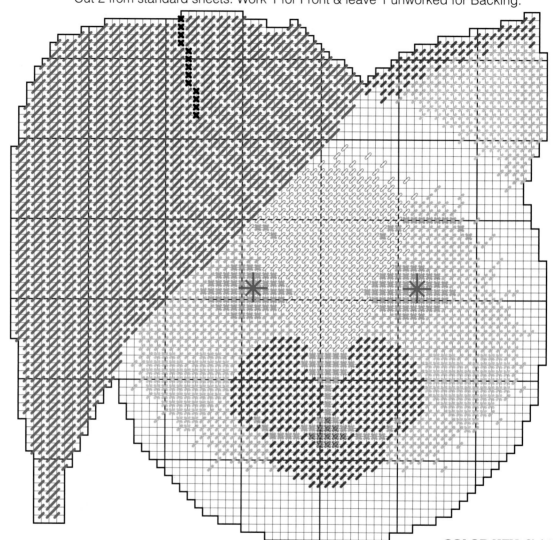

D – Bow Loop
(47w x 11h-hole pieces) Cut 4 from standard sheet & work.

Whipstitch

Whipstitch

Fold line

COLOR KEY: Christmas Kitt[e]

	Worsted-weight	YARN AMOUNT
	Dk. Green	2¹/₂ oz. [70.9g
	Green	46 yds. [42.1m
	White	40 yds. [36.6m
	Sandstone	15 yds. [13.7m
	Red	13 yds. [11.9m
	Black	8 yds. [7.3m]
	Maple	6 yds. [5.5m]
	Camel	5 yds. [4.6m]
	Pink	5 yds. [4.6m]
	Eggshell	4 yds. [3.7m]
	Burgundy	1 yd. [0.9m]
	Watermelon	1 yd. [0.9m]

STITCH KEY:

− Straight

✳ Smyrna Cross

B – Paw
(19w x 12h-hole pieces)
Cut 2 from standard sheet & work.

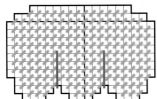

C – Package Front & Backing
(90w x 90h-hole pieces)
Cut 2 from large sheets. Work 1 for Front & leave 1 unworked for Backing.

Holly Accents

Coordinate your holiday decor with this holly trio.

SIZES: Basket is 7¾" square x about 10"
tall [19.7cm x 25.4cm], including Handle;
Ornament Topper covers a 2½" [6.4cm]
Christmas ball ornament; Stocking is 7½" x
9¾" [19cm x 24.8cm].

SKILL LEVEL: Challenging

MATERIALS:
Three sheets of 7-mesh QuickCount®
plastic canvas by Uniek, Inc.
One 2½" [6.4cm] Christmas ball ornament
Three 8" square [20.3cm] sheets of red felt
1 yd. [0.9m] of red ⅛" [3mm] satin ribbon
One women's size 9-12 white nylon sock
Craft glue or glue gun
Metallic Needloft® craft cord by Uniek;
for amount see Color Key.
Worsted-weight or Needloft® plastic
canvas yarn by Uniek, Inc.; for amounts
see Color Key.

CUTTING INSTRUCTIONS:
A: For Basket Sides, cut four 51w x
55h-holes.
B: For Basket Bottom, cut one 51w x 51h-
holes (no graph).
C: For Basket Handle Pieces, cut two 64w
x 5h-holes (no graph).
D: For Holly Leaves #1 and #2, cut number
indicated according to graphs.
E: For Holly Berries, cut five according
to graph.
F: For Stocking Front, cut one according
to graph.
G: For Ornament Topper, cut one
according to graph.

STITCHING INSTRUCTIONS:
NOTE: B is not worked.
1: Using colors and stitches indicated, work

A and D-G pieces according to graphs.
Overlapping eight holes at one end of each
Handle Piece and working through both
thicknesses at overlap area to join, using
white and slanted gobelin stitch over narrow width, work C pieces, forming Handle
assembly. With matching colors, overcast
edges of D, E and G pieces; with red,
overcast long edges of Handle assembly.
NOTE: For Basket Linings, using A-C
pieces as patterns, cut one each from felt
⅛" [3mm] smaller at all edges.
2: With matching colors, whipstitch A and
B pieces together, forming Basket; with red,
overcast unfinished edges, catching ends of
Handle assembly to Basket at opposite
Sides as indicated on A graph (see photo)
as you work. Glue linings inside Basket
and to wrong side of Basket Handle.
3: Glue one Holly Leaf #2 to each Basket
Side over Handle (see photo) and one Holly
Leaf #1 to each remaining Basket Side (see
photo); glue one Holly Berry to each Holly
Leaf cluster around Basket as shown.
NOTE: For Stocking Backing, using G as a
pattern, cut one from sock ⅛" [3mm] larger
at all edges. Fold over raw edges ¼" [6mm]
and with iron set on low heat, press to
form seam.
4: Holding Stocking Backing to wrong side
of F with seam edges between, with green,
whipstitch together as indicated; with red,
overcast unfinished top edges of F.
5: Tie ribbon into a multi-loop bow; glue
bow and remaining Holly Leaf #1 and
Holly Berry to Stocking as shown in photo.
Hang as desired. Insert cutout of Ornament
Topper through hanger on Christmas
ornament (see photo); glue Topper to
ornament to secure.

—Designed by Sandra Miller Maxfield

JOLLY HOLLY

A – Basket Side (51w x 26h-hole pieces) Cut 4 & work.

Handle Attachment

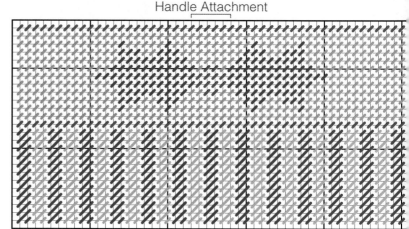

COLOR KEY: Holly Accents

Metallic cord	Need-loft®	AMOUNT
■ Solid Gold	#55020	3 yds. [3.7m]

Worsted-weight	Need-loft®	YARN AMOUNT
■ Holly	#27	3 oz. [85.1g]
■ Mermaid	#53	55 yds. [50.3m]
■ White	#41	55 yds. [50.3m]
■ Red	#01	40 yds. [36.6m]

STITCH KEY:
⊟ Backstitch/Straight

F – Stocking Front
(51w x 66h-hole piece) Cut 1 & work.

Whipstitch to Stocking Backing between arrows.

E – Holly Berry
(4w x 4h-hole pieces) Cut 5 & work.

G – Ornament Topper
(19w x 19h-hole piece) Cut 1 & work.

Cut out gray area.

D – Holly Leaf #1
(26w x 7h-hole pieces) Cut 3 & wo|

D – Holly Leaf #2
(27w x 18h-hole pieces) Cut 2 & work.

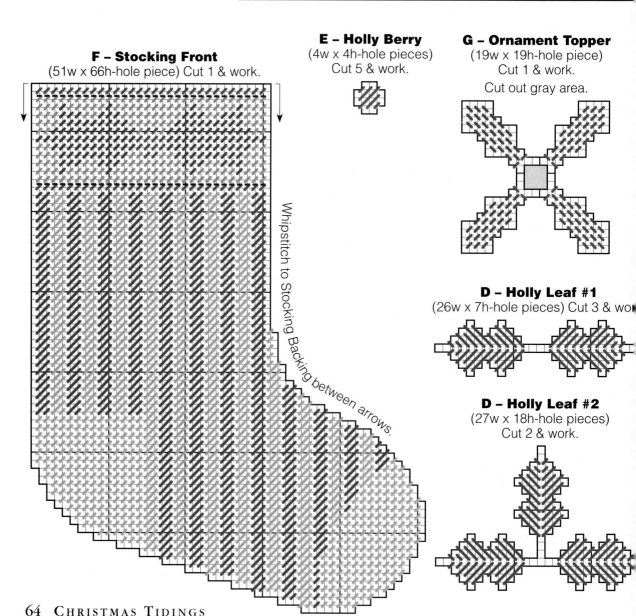

Christmas Joy Blocks

Display your feelings of
the season with these colorful blocks.

SIZE: Each is 2" [5.1cm] square.

SKILL LEVEL: Easy

MATERIALS:

One Sheet of QuickCount® 7-mesh
Plastic Canvas by Uniek, Inc.
Needloft® Yarn by Uniek, Inc. or worsted
yarn; for amounts see Color Key.

CUTTING INSTRUCTIONS:

A: For "J" Sides, cut six 12w x 12h-holes.
B: For "O" Sides, cut six 12w x 12h-holes.
C: For "Y" Sides, cut six 12w x 12h-holes.

STITCHING INSTRUCTIONS:

1: Using colors indicated and continental
stitch, work pieces according to graphs.
2: With eggshell, whipstitch A pieces
together, forming "J" Block; repeat with B
pieces, forming "O" Block and C pieces,
forming "Y" Block. Display as desired.

—Designed by Angie Arickx

COLOR KEY: Christmas Joy Blocks

Worsted-weight	Need-loft®	YARN AMOUNT
☒ Eggshell	#39	28 yds. [25.6m]
■ Forest	#29	17 yds. [15.5m]
■ Burgundy	#03	10 yds. [9.1m]

A – "J" Side
(12w x 12h-hole pieces)
Cut 6 & work.

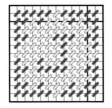

B – "O" Side
(12w x 12h-hole pieces)
Cut 6 & work.

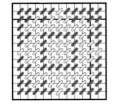

C – "Y" Side
(12w x 12h-hole pieces)
Cut 6 & work.

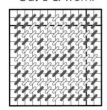

Music Button Covers

*Quick-to-make musical ornaments
are sure to enhance your seasonal furnishings.*

SIZE: Each holds a 1½" [3.8cm] music button.

SKILL LEVEL: Challenging

MATERIALS:
- One sheet of 14-mesh plastic canvas
- Six 1½" [3.8cm] music buttons with Christmas melodies of choice
- Six-strand metallic embroidery floss; for amount see Color Key.
  - Six-strand cotton embroidery floss; for amounts see Color Key.
  - 3-ply or sport weight yarn; for amounts see Color Key

CUTTING INSTRUCTIONS:
A: For Cover Fronts, cut one each according to graphs.
B: For Cover Backs, cut six (one for each Cover) according to graph.
C: For Cover Bands, cut six (one for each Cover) 72w x 6h-holes (no graph).

STITCHING INSTRUCTIONS
1: Using colors and stitches indicated, work A and B pieces according to graphs. F in uncoded areas of "Tree," "Cardinal," "Sleigh," "Train" and "Poinsettia" A pieces usir white yarn and continental stitch; fill in uncoded areas of "Candle" A using green yarn and continental stitch.
2: Using green yarn and continental stitch, work four C pieces; using red and white yarn and continental stitch, work one remaining C in eac color. For each Band (make 6), with yarn color to match color of Band, whipstitch

short ends of one C wrong sides together.

Using cotton and metallic floss and yarn in colors and embroidery stitches indicated, embroider detail on A pieces as indicated on graphs.

For each Cover (make 6), with yarn color to match Band, whipstitch one A and one of each desired-color B and C pieces together, inserting music button (**NOTE:** Place silver side of music button on wrong side of .) before closing.

Decorate and hang Music Button Covers as desired.

—Designed by Nancy Dorman

A – "Train" Front
(22w x 22h-hole piece)
Cut 1 & work.

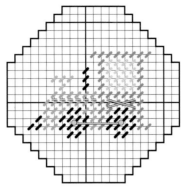

A – "Tree" Front
(22w x 22h-hole piece)
Cut 1 & work.

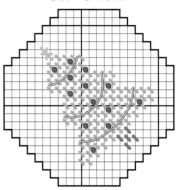

A – "Poinsettia" Front
(22w x 22h-hole piece)
Cut 1 & work.

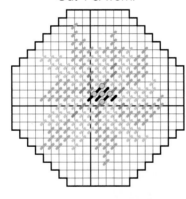

A – "Candle" Front
(22w x 22h-hole piece)
Cut 1 & work.

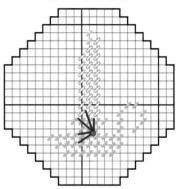

A – "Cardinal" Front
(22w x 22h-hole piece)
Cut 1 & work.

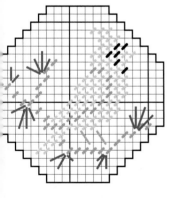

A – "Sleigh" Front
(22w x 22h-hole piece)
Cut 1 & work.

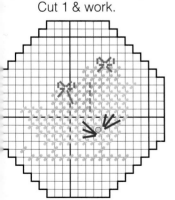

COLOR KEY: Music Button Covers

Cotton floss	AMOUNT
■ 2-strand Forest	2 yds. [1.8m]
■ 2-strand Green	1 yd. [0.9m]
■ 2-strand Red	1 yd. [0.9m]
■ 2-strand White	1/4 yd. [0.2m]

Metallic floss	AMOUNT
▨ 6-strand Gold	4 yds. [3.7m]
⊘ 2-strand Gold	2 yds. [1.8m]

Sport-weight	YARN AMOUNT
▨ Green	72 yds. [65.8m]
⊘ White	40 yds. [36.6m]
▨ Red	25 yds. [22.9m]
▨ Burgundy	2 yds. [1.8m]
■ Black	1 yd. [0.9m]
▨ Camel	1 yd. [0.9m]
▨ Gray	1/2 yd. [0.5m]
▨ Brown	1/4 yd. [0.2m]
▨ Tan	1/4 yd. [0.2m]

STITCH KEY:
- ▬ Backstitch/Straight
- ● French Knot

B – Cover Back
(22w x 22h-hole pieces)
Cut 6. Work 4; substituting white & red for green, work 1 in each color.

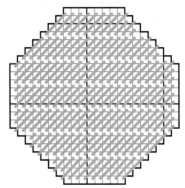

Candy Cane Container

Give a gift of Christmas
goodies in this festive holiday container.

SIZE: Snugly conceals a 1-lb. coffee can.

SKILL LEVEL: Average

MATERIALS:
- One Sheet of QuickCount® 7-mesh Plastic Canvas by Uniek, Inc.
- One of each QuickShape™ 6" [15.2cm] and 4" [10.2cm] Plastic Canvas Radial Circle by Uniek, Inc.

- Craft glue or glue gun
- Needloft® Yarn by Uniek, Inc. or worste yarn; for amounts see Color Key.

CUTTING INSTRUCTIONS:
A: For Side, cut one 87w x 35h-holes.
B: For Bottom, use 4" circle (no graph).
C: For Lid Top, cut one from 6" circle according to graph.
D: For Lid Rim cut one 77w x 3h-holes (no graph).
E: For Holly, cut one according to graph.

STITCHING INSTRUCTIONS:
NOTE: B is not worked.
1: Using colors and stitches indicated, wor A, C and E pieces according to graphs; work D using white and slanted gobelin stitch over narrow width. Fill in uncoded areas of A using holly and continental stitch. With forest for Lid Top and with matching colors as shown in photo, overcast edges of C and E pieces.
2: Using black (Separate into individual plies, if desired.) and backstitch, embroide detail on A as indicated on graph.
3: With holly, whipstitch short edges of A together; with forest, whipstitch A and B pieces together, forming Container. Overcast unfinished top edges. With white whipstitch short edges of D wrong sides together, forming Lid Rim; overcast unfinished edges.
4: Glue Lid Rim to center wrong side of Lid Top; glue Holly to right side of Lid Top as shown.

—Designed by Mike Vicke

E – Holly
(28w x 13h-hole piece)
Cut 1 & work.

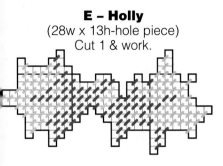

C – Lid Top
(6" circle)
Cut away gray area & work.

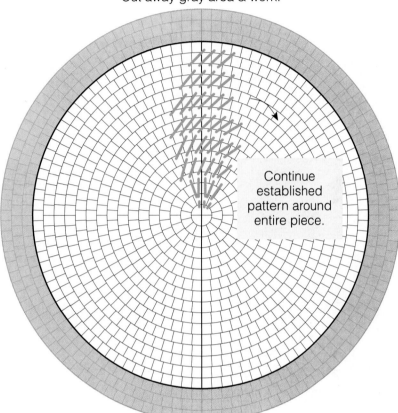

Continue established pattern around entire piece.

COLOR KEY: Candy Cane Container

Worsted-weight	Need-loft®	YARN AMOUNT
Holly	#27	55 yds. [50.3m]
White	#41	32 yds. [29.3m]
Forest	#29	30 yds. [27.4m]
Red	#01	14 yds. [12.8m]
Burgundy	#03	10 yds. [9.1m]
Silver	#37	10 yds. [9.1m]
Black	#00	8 yds. [7.3m]

STITCH KEY:
– Backstitch/Straight

A – Side
(87w x 35h-hole piece) Cut 1 & work.

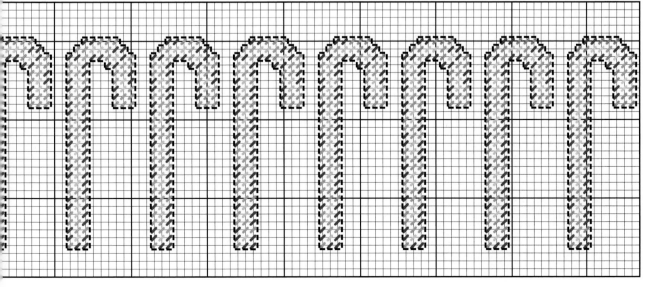

Holiday Table Runner

Make your table the center
of attention with this fabulous runner.

SIZE: 11¼" x 21¾" [28.6cm x 55.2cm], not including holly leaves.

SKILL LEVEL: Average

MATERIALS:
One 13½" x 21½" [34.3cm x 54.6cm] Sheet and ½ Sheet of Standard-size 7-mesh QuickCount® Plastic Canvas by Uniek, Inc.
Four red 10mm round faceted beads
Sewing needle and black thread
Craft glue or glue gun
Fine (#8) Metallic Braid by Kreinik Mfg. Co. or six-strand metallic embroidery floss; for amount see Color Key.
Needloft® Yarn by Uniek, Inc. or worsted yarn; for amounts see Color Key.

CUTTING INSTRUCTIONS:
A: For Table Runner, cut one according to graph.
B: For Holly Leaf Motifs, cut four according to graph.

STITCHING INSTRUCTIONS:
1: Using colors and stitches indicated, work pieces according to graphs; with matching colors, overcast edges of pieces.
2: With sewing needle and thread, sew one bead to center right side of each B as indicated on graph. Glue one Holly Leaf Motif to each corner of Table Runner as shown in photo.

—Designed by Kristine Loffredo

COLOR KEY: Holiday Table Runner

Braid or floss	Kreinik	AMOUNT
Gold	#002C	3 yds. [3.7m]

Worsted-weight	Needloft®	YARN AMOUNT
Forest	#29	50 yds. [45.7m]
Burgundy	#03	48 yds. [43.9m]
Christmas Green	#28	16 yds. [14.6m]
Flesh Tone	#56	15 yds. [13.7m]

ATTACHMENT KEY:
◙ Bead

B – Holly Leaf Motif
(32w x 14h-hole pieces)
Cut 4 from standard sheet & work.

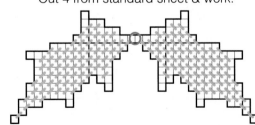

COLOR KEY: Holiday Table Runner

Braid or floss	Kreinik	AMOUNT
Gold	#002C	3 yds. [3.7m]

Worsted-weight	Need-loft®	YARN AMOUNT
Forest	#29	50 yds. [45.7m]
Burgundy	#03	48 yds. [43.9m]
Christmas Green	#28	16 yds. [14.6m]
Flesh Tone	#56	15 yds. [13.7m]

ATTACHMENT KEY:

O Bead

A – Table Runner
(145w x 75h-hole piece) Cut 1 from large sheet & work.

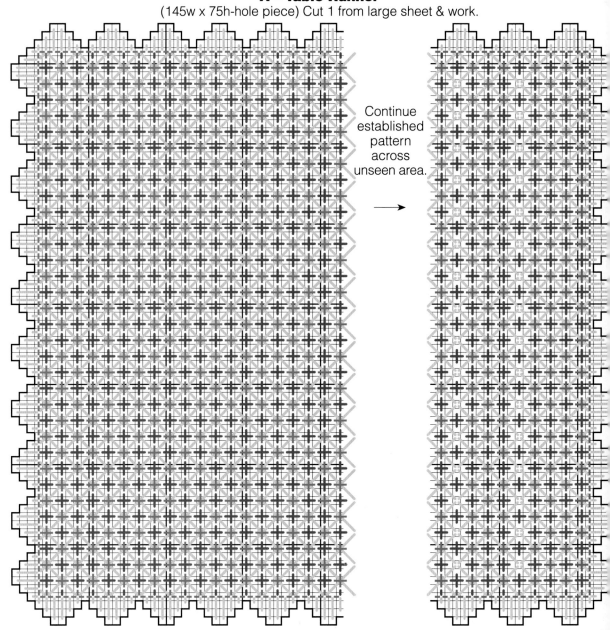

Continue established pattern across unseen area.

→

Striped Tissue Cover

Conceal a tissue box while adding
a touch of holiday elegance to your decor.

SIZE: Snugly covers a boutique-style tissue box.

SKILL LEVEL: Easy

MATERIALS:
Two sheets of 7-mesh plastic canvas
Four silk holly clusters with berries
Craft glue or glue gun
Metallic cord; for amounts see Color Key.
Worsted-weight or plastic canvas yarn; for amount see Color Key.

CUTTING INSTRUCTIONS:
NOTE: Graphs continued on page 76.
A: For Lid Top, cut one according to graph.
B: For Lid Sides, cut four 33w x 7h-holes.
C: For Box Sides, cut four 30w x 36h-holes.
D: For Box Bottom, cut one 33w x 33h-holes (no graph).

STITCHING INSTRUCTIONS:
NOTE: D is not worked.
1: Using colors and stitches indicated, work A-C pieces according to graphs; with white, overcast cutout edges of A.
2: With white, whipstitch A and B pieces together, forming Lid; whipstitch C and D pieces together, forming Box. Overcast unfinished edges of Lid and Box.
NOTE: Cut red cord in half; tie each length into a multi-looped bow.
3: Glue bows and holly clusters to Lid as shown in photo.

—Designed by Susie Spier Maxfield

COLOR KEY: Striped Tissue Cover	
Metallic cord	**AMOUNT**
▩ Gold	42 yds. [38.4m]
☐ Red	2 yds. [1.8m]
Worsted-weight	**YARN AMOUNT**
▨ White	70 yds. [64m]

B – Lid Side
(33w x 7h-hole pieces) Cut 4 & work.

Mantel Runner

Cover your mantel with this holly
trimmed runner for a great yuletide look.

SIZE: 1½" x 6" x 35¼" long [3.8cm x 15.2cm x 89.5cm].

SKILL LEVEL: Challenging

MATERIALS:
- Two 13½" x 21½" [34.3cm x 54.6cm] sheets of 7-mesh QuickCount® Plastic Canvas by Uniek, Inc.
- 39 dk. red 6mm round faceted beads
- Sewing needle and black thread
- Metallic cord; for amount see Color Key.
- Worsted-weight or Needloft® plastic canvas yarn by Uniek, Inc.; for amounts see Color Key.

CUTTING INSTRUCTIONS:
A: For Top Piece #1, cut one 117w x 39h-holes.
B: For Top Piece #2, cut one 121w x 39h-holes.
C: For Front Pieces #1 and #2, cut one each according to graphs.

STITCHING INSTRUCTIONS:
1: Using colors and stitches indicated, work pieces according to graphs. With green, overcast edges of C pieces.
2: Using sewing needle and black thread, sew three beads to each ▲ hole on C pieces as indicated on graphs (see photo). With forest, overcast edges of A pieces, attaching C pieces to one long edge of A at each ◆ hole as indicated as you work.

—Designed by Kristine Loffred

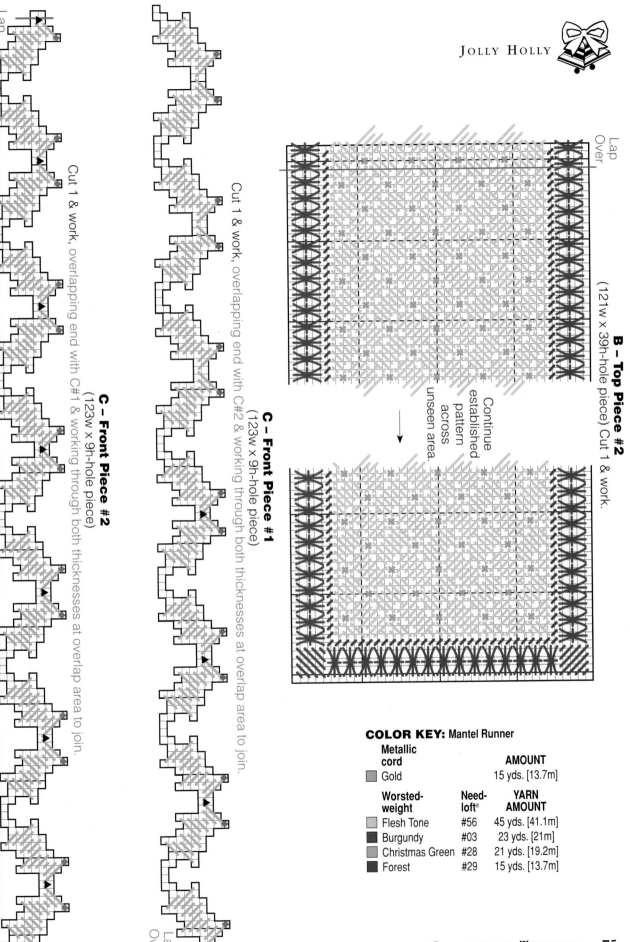

B – Top Piece #2
(121w x 39h-hole piece) Cut 1 & work.

Lap
Over

Continue
established
pattern
across
unseen area.

Cut 1 & work, overlapping end with C#1 & working through both thicknesses at overlap area to join.

C – Front Piece #2
(123w x 9h-hole piece)

Cut 1 & work, overlapping end with C#2 & working through both thicknesses at overlap area to join.

C – Front Piece #1
(123w x 9h-hole piece)

Lap
Over

Lap
Over

COLOR KEY: Mantel Runner

Metallic cord		AMOUNT
Gold		15 yds. [13.7m]

Worsted-weight	Need-loft®	YARN AMOUNT
Flesh Tone	#56	45 yds. [41.1m]
Burgundy	#03	23 yds. [21m]
Christmas Green	#28	21 yds. [19.2m]
Forest	#29	15 yds. [13.7m]

A – Top Piece #1
(117w x 39h-hole piece) Cut 1 & work.

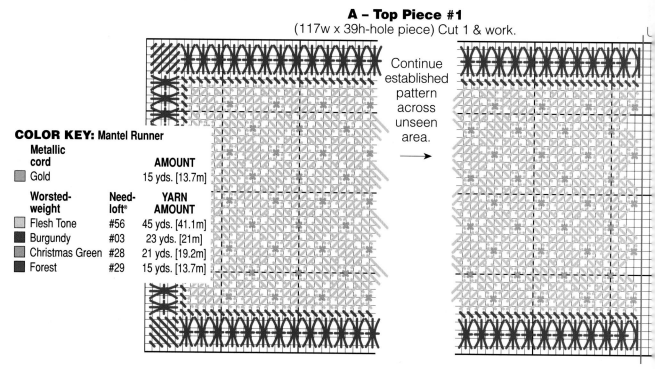

Continue established pattern across unseen area.

→

COLOR KEY: Mantel Runner

Metallic cord		AMOUNT
Gold		15 yds. [13.7m]

Worsted-weight	Need-loft®	YARN AMOUNT
Flesh Tone	#56	45 yds. [41.1m]
Burgundy	#03	23 yds. [21m]
Christmas Green	#28	21 yds. [19.2m]
Forest	#29	15 yds. [13.7m]

Striped Tissue Cover
Instructions on page 73

COLOR KEY: Striped Tissue Cover

Metallic cord	AMOUNT
Gold	42 yds. [38.4m]
Red	2 yds. [1.8m]

Worsted-weight	YARN AMOUNT
White	70 yds. [64m]

C – Box Side
(30w x 36h-hole pieces) Cut 4 & work.

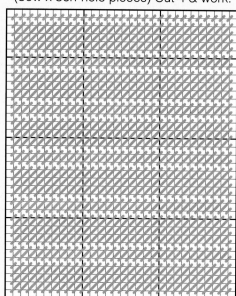

A – Lid Top
(33w x 33h-hole piece) Cut 1 & work.

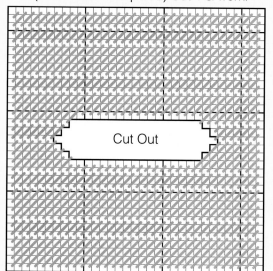

Cut Out

Christmas Place Mat

*Dine in the spirit of the season
with this holly embellished place mat.*

SIZE: 12" x 17½" [30.5cm x 44.5cm].

MATERIALS:
One sheet of 13½" x 21½" [34.3cm x
54.6cm] 7-mesh plastic canvas
Metallic Braid Ribbon by GlissenGloss™
(for amounts see Color Key on page 78).
Red Heart® Super Saver® Art E300 by
Coats & Clark or worsted yarn (for
amounts see Color Key).

CUTTING INSTRUCTIONS:
For Place Mat, cut one according to graph.

STITCHING INSTRUCTIONS:
1: Using colors and stitches indicated, work
piece according to graph.
2: With white yarn, overcast edges.

—Designed by Marlene Hippen

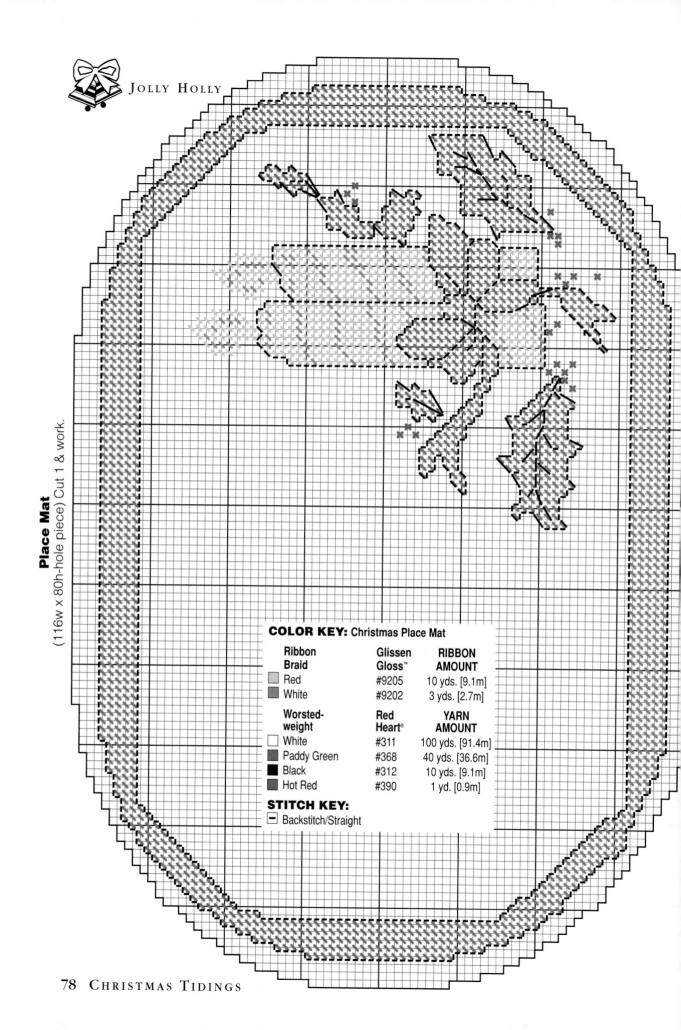

JOLLY HOLLY

Place Mat
(116w x 80h-hole piece) Cut 1 & work.

COLOR KEY: Christmas Place Mat

Ribbon Braid	Glissen Gloss™	RIBBON AMOUNT
Red	#9205	10 yds. [9.1m]
White	#9202	3 yds. [2.7m]

Worsted-weight	Red Heart®	YARN AMOUNT
White	#311	100 yds. [91.4m]
Paddy Green	#368	40 yds. [36.6m]
Black	#312	10 yds. [9.1m]
Hot Red	#390	1 yd. [0.9m]

STITCH KEY:
⊟ Backstitch/Straight

CHAPTER FOUR

Nutcracker Suite

"Toyland, toyland, little girl and boy land" . . . light up young faces this holiday season with an army of toy soldiers. This collection of bright colors, cheerful shapes and whimsical childlike designs are sure to bring out the kid in all of us.

Nutcracker Doorstop

*This guy is sure to stand at
attention as he greets your guests this season.*

SIZE: 2¾" x 5" x 10½" tall [7cm x 12.7cm x 26.7cm].

SKILL LEVEL: Average

MATERIALS:
- Two Sheets of QuickCount® 7-mesh Plastic Canvas by Uniek, Inc.
- Two yellow ½" [13mm] sew-on buttons
- Sewing needle
- Zip-close bag filled with gravel or other weighting material
- Craft glue or glue gun
- No. 5 Pearl Cotton (Coton Perlé) Art. 116 by DMC® or six-strand embroidery floss; for amounts see Color Key.
- Needloft® Yarn by Uniek, Inc. or worsted yarn; for amounts see Color Key.

CUTTING INSTRUCTIONS:
A: For Motif, cut one according to graph.
B: For Cover Sides, cut two 26w x 51h-holes (no graph).
C: For Cover Ends, cut two 16w x 51h-holes (no graph).
D: For Cover Top & Bottom, cut two (one for Top and one for Bottom) 26w x 16h-holes (no graph).

...ITCHING INSTRUCTIONS:

...: Using colors and stitches indicated, work
...according to graph and B-D pieces
...ccording to Cover Stitch Pattern Guide.
...ith matching colors, overcast edges of A.
...: Using pearl cotton or three strands floss
...colors and embroidery stitches indicated,
...mbroider detail on A as indicated on
...aph. With sewing needle and lt. lemon

pearl cotton or floss, sew buttons to A
as indicated.

3: For Cover, with gold, whipstitch B-D
pieces wrong sides together, inserting
weighting material before closing. Matching
bottom edges, glue Motif to one Cover
Side (see photo).

—Designed by Michele Wilcox

Cover Stitch Pattern Guide

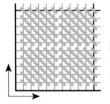

Continue
established
pattern up &
across each
entire piece.

COLOR KEY: Nutcracker Doorstop

Pearl cotton or floss	DMC®	AMOUNT
■ Black	#310	1 yd. [0.9m]
▨ Lt. Lemon	#445	1 yd. [0.9m]

Worsted-weight	Need-loft®	YARN AMOUNT
▨ Gold	#17	70 yds. [64m]
▨ Royal	#32	15 yds. [13.7m]
▨ Red	#01	7 yds. [6.4m]
▨ Black	#00	6 yds. [5.5m]
▨ White	#41	4 yds. [3.7m]
▨ Beige	#40	3 yds. [2.7m]
▨ Yellow	#57	3 yds. [2.7m]

OTHER:

- ⊟ Backstitch/Straight
- ⦿ French Knot
- ◆ Button Attachment

A – Motif
(33w x 69h-hole piece)
Cut 1 & work.

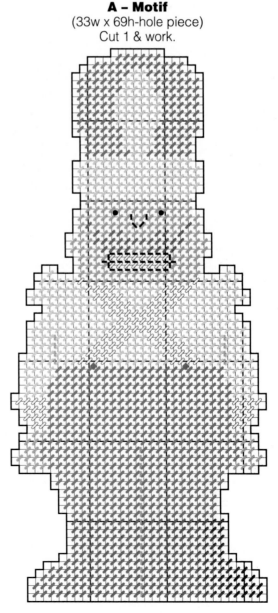

Treat Holder

A pocket full of Christmas cheer
can be yours with this adorable treat holder.

SIZE: 2⅛" x 6½" x 6½" tall [5.4cm x 16.5cm x 16.5cm].

SKILL LEVEL: Average

MATERIALS:
- One Sheet of QuickCount® 7-mesh Plastic Canvas by Uniek, Inc.
- Craft glue or glue gun
- Metallic cord; for amount see Color Key.
- Needloft® Yarn by Uniek, Inc. or worsted yarn; for amounts see Color Key.

CUTTING INSTRUCTIONS:
A: For Back, cut one according to graph.
B: For Sides, cut two according to graph.
C: For Front and Bottom, cut two (one for Front and one for Bottom) according to graph.
D: For Hat Brim, cut one according to graph.
E: For Nose, cut one according to graph.
F: For Arms #1 and #2, cut one each according to graphs.
G: For Feet, cut two according to graph.
H: For Holly, cut one according to graph.

STITCHING INSTRUCTIONS:
NOTE: One C is not worked for Bottom.
1: Using colors and stitches indicated, work pieces according to graphs. Omitting attachment edges, with indicated and matching colors, overcast edges of A and D-H pieces.
2: Using metallic cord and yarn (Separate yarn into individual plies, if desired.) in colors and embroidery stitches indicated, embroider detail on A as indicated on graph.
3: With Christmas green, whipstitch B and Front C pieces wrong sides together and to right side of A as indicated. Whipstitch Bottom C to assembly; overcast unfinished edges of B and Front C pieces.
4: With matching colors, whipstitch D-F pieces to right side of A as indicated (see photo). Glue Arms to Sides and wrong side of one Foot to each leg on right side of Back as shown in photo. Glue Holly to Front as shown.

—Designed by Kristine Loffred

B – Side
(17w x 17h-hole pieces)
Cut 2 & work.

A – Back
(45w x 45h-hole piece)
Cut 1 & work.

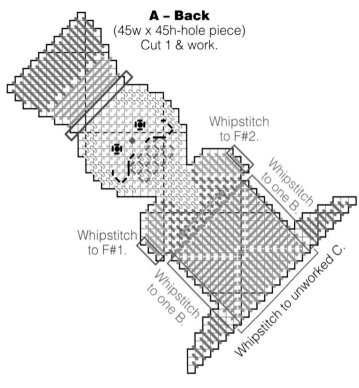

Whipstitch to F#2.

Whipstitch to F#1.

Whipstitch to one B.

Whipstitch to one B.

Whipstitch to unworked C.

C – Front & Bottom
(18w x 18h-hole pieces)
Cut 2. Work 1 for Front &
leave 1 unworked for Bottom.

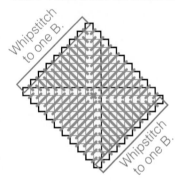

Whipstitch to one B.

Whipstitch to one B.

E – Nose
(3w x 3h-hole piece)
Cut 1 & work.

Whipstitch to A.

D – Hat Brim
(9w x 9h-hole piece)
Cut 1 & work.

Whipstitch to A.

G – Foot
(6w x 13h-hole pieces)
Cut 2 & work.

COLOR KEY: Treat Holder

Metallic cord		AMOUNT
Gold		2 yds. [1.8m]

Worsted-weight	Need-loft®	YARN AMOUNT
Christmas Green	#28	10 yds. [9.1m]
Black	#00	4 yds. [3.7m]
Christmas Red	#02	3 yds. [2.7m]
Pink	#07	3 yds. [2.7m]
Royal	#32	3 yds. [2.7m]
White	#41	2 yds. [1.8m]
Fern	#23	1 yd. 0.9m]

OTHER:
- Backstitch/Straight
- French Knot
- Nose Attachment
- Hat Brim/Back
- Arms/Back
- Side/Back
- Side/Front

F – Arm #1 & #2
(5w x 13h-hole pieces)
Cut 1 each & work.

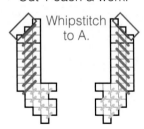

Whipstitch to A.

H – Holly
(9w x 5h-hole piece)
Cut 1 & work.

Overcast with
Christmas Red.

Toy Soldier

Complete your toyland theme by putting this soldier in charge.

ZES: Soldier is 4⅞" x 12¾" [12.4cm x 2.4cm]; Stand is 3" x 4⅝" x 1" tall [7.6cm x 1.7cm x 2.5cm].

KILL LEVEL: Challenging

MATERIALS:
One Sheet of QuickCount® Clear Stiff and One Sheet of 7-mesh Plastic Canvas by Uniek, Inc.
Two ⅜" [10mm] decorative shank buttons
11 Gold ⅜" [10mm] Star Charms by Creative Beginnings
13 gold 4mm beads
⅛ yd. [0.1m] white 1" [2.5cm] eyelet lace
¼ yd. [0.2m] gold ½" [13mm] gold decorative braid trim
One red 2"-long [5.1cm] artificial feather
⅛ yd. [0.1m] white ¼" [6mm] satin ribbon
One 1" x 2¾" x 4⅜" [2.5cm x 7cm x 11.1cm] block of Styrofoam®
Sewing needle and red, white, black and gold sewing thread
Craft glue or glue gun
Needloft® Craft Cord by Uniek, Inc.; for amount see Color Key.
Needloft® Yarn by Uniek, Inc. or worsted yarn; for amounts see Color Key.

CUTTING INSTRUCTIONS:
: For Soldier Front, cut one according to graph.
: For Soldier Back, cut one according to graph.
: For Stand Top, cut one according to graph.
D: For Stand Sides, cut two 30w x 6h-holes.
: For Stand Ends, cut two 19w x 6h-holes.

STITCHING INSTRUCTIONS:
: Using colors and stitches indicated, work pieces according to graphs. With black, overcast cutout edges of C.
: Using cord and yarn (Separate yarn into individual plies, if desired.) and embroidery stitches indicated, embroider detail on A as indicated on graph.

3: With red thread, sew one star charm to each ♥ hole on A as indicated. With black thread, sew one star charm to each ◆ hole on D and E pieces as indicated. Thread feather through shank of one button; with black thread, sew button (over feather) to ▲ hole on A as indicated to secure. With gold thread, sew beads to A as indicated.
4: For medal, fold under short ends of white ribbon ⅛" [3mm]; with white thread, sew to secure. Sew remaining star to one end of ribbon. Hold opposite ribbon end to ▼ hole on A as indicated; sew remaining decorative button to A over ribbon end to secure.
5: With matching colors, whipstitch A and B pieces wrong sides together. With black, whipstitch short ends of D and E pieces wrong sides together. Whipstitch assembly to wrong side of C, forming Stand; overcast unfinished edges.
6: For ascot, fold lace several times (see photo) and with white thread, sew together to secure; sew remaining bead to ascot as shown. Glue ascot to Soldier's neck (see photo). Glue braid around Soldier's shoulders as shown in photo, trimming as needed to fit.
7: Insert foam block inside Stand; insert Soldier through opening in Stand and push into foam block for stability.

—Designed by Ronda Bryce

COLOR KEY: Toy Soldier

Metallic cord	Need-loft®	CORD AMOUNT
Gold	#01	1 yd. [0.9m]

Worsted-weight	Need-loft®	YARN AMOUNT
Black	#00	41 yds. [37.5m]
Red	#01	20 yds. [18.3m]
Royal	#32	14 yds. [12.8m]
Burgundy	#03	12 yds. [11m]
Dark Royal	#48	7 yds. [6.4m]
Beige	#40	4 yds. [3.7m]
Cinnamon	#14	1 yd. [0.9m]

OTHER:
▬ Backstitch/Straight
◎ Bead Attachment

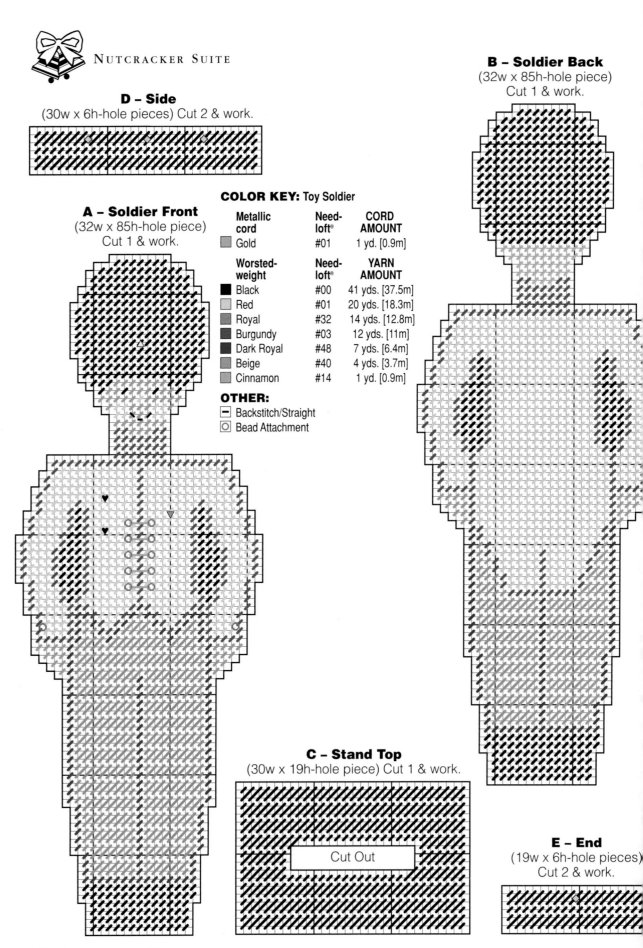

B – Soldier Back
(32w x 85h-hole piece)
Cut 1 & work.

D – Side
(30w x 6h-hole pieces) Cut 2 & work.

A – Soldier Front
(32w x 85h-hole piece)
Cut 1 & work.

COLOR KEY: Toy Soldier

Metallic cord	Need-loft®	CORD AMOUNT
Gold	#01	1 yd. [0.9m]

Worsted-weight	Need-loft®	YARN AMOUNT
Black	#00	41 yds. [37.5m]
Red	#01	20 yds. [18.3m]
Royal	#32	14 yds. [12.8m]
Burgundy	#03	12 yds. [11m]
Dark Royal	#48	7 yds. [6.4m]
Beige	#40	4 yds. [3.7m]
Cinnamon	#14	1 yd. [0.9m]

OTHER:
- Backstitch/Straight
- Bead Attachment

C – Stand Top
(30w x 19h-hole piece) Cut 1 & work.

Cut Out

E – End
(19w x 6h-hole pieces)
Cut 2 & work.

Napkin Ring

Add an extra accent to your table setting with this festive toy soldier.

SIZE: 2¼" x 3¾" [5.7cm x 9.5cm].

SKILL LEVEL: Easy

MATERIALS:
One Sheet of QuickCount® 7-mesh Plastic Canvas by Uniek, Inc.
Craft glue or glue gun
Metallic cord; for amount see Color Key.
Needloft® Yarn by Uniek, Inc. or worsted yarn; for amounts see Color Key.

CUTTING INSTRUCTIONS:
A: For Body, cut one according to graph.
B: For Hat Brim, cut one according to graph.
C: For Beard, cut one according to graph.
D: For Napkin Band, cut one 44w x 4h-holes.

STITCHING INSTRUCTIONS:
1: Using colors and stitches indicated, work pieces according to graphs. With matching colors, overcast edges of A, C and D pieces; omitting attachment edges, with black, overcast edges of B.

2: Using yarn (Separate into individual plies, if desired.) in colors and embroidery stitches indicated, embroider detail on A as indicated on graph.
3: With black, whipstitch B to right side of A as indicated. Glue Beard top as indicated to right side of Body and Body to Napkin Band as shown in photo.

—Designed by Kristine Loffredo

COLOR KEY: Napkin Ring

Metallic cord	Need-loft®	CORD AMOUNT
Gold	#01	1 yd. [0.9m]

Worsted-weight	Need-loft®	YARN AMOUNT
Red	#01	4 yds. [3.7m]
Royal	#32	2 yds. [1.8m]
Black	#00	1 yd. [0.9m]
Cinnamon	#14	1 yd. [0.9m]
Orchid	#44	1 yd. [0.9m]
White	#41	1 yd. [0.9m]

OTHER:
| Backstitch/Straight
| French Knot
| Hat Brim Attachment

B – Hat Brim
(7w x 2h-hole piece)
Cut 1 & work.
Whipstitch to A.

C – Beard
(3w x 3h-hole piece)
Cut 1 & work.

A – Body
(9w x 25h-hole piece)
Cut 1 & work.

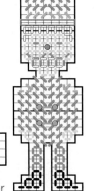

D – Napkin Band
(44w x 4h-hole piece)
Cut 1 & work, overlapping ends & working through both thicknesses at overlap area to join.

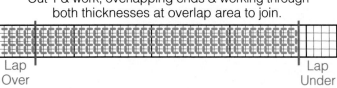

Lap Over   Lap Under

Stocking

Naughty or nice, this soldier will see that your stocking is filled tonight.

SIZE: 1" x 6½" x 14¼" [2.5cm x 16.5cm x 36.2cm].

SKILL LEVEL: Average

MATERIALS:
- One Sheet of QuickCount® 7-mesh Plastic Canvas by Uniek, Inc.

- ½ yd. [0.5m] natural raffia
- Craft glue or glue gun
- Needloft® Craft Cord by Uniek, Inc.; for amount see Color Key.
- Needloft® Yarn by Uniek, Inc. or worsted yarn; for amounts see Color Key.

CUTTING INSTRUCTIONS:
NOTE: Graphs continued on page 91.
A: For Back, cut one according to graph.
B: For Front, cut one according to graph.
C: For Hat Plume, cut one according to graph.
D: For Hat Brim, cut one according to graph.
E: For Nose, cut one according to graph.
F: For Beard, cut one according to graph.
G: For Hands, cut one each according to graphs.

STITCHING INSTRUCTIONS:
1: Using colors and stitches indicated, work pieces according to graphs. Omitting attachment edges, with matching colors, overcast edges of pieces.
2: Using yarn (Separate into individual plies, if desired.) in colors and embroidery stitches indicated, embroider detail on A as indicated on graph.
3: With matching colors, whipstitch D-F pieces to right side of A as indicated; holding B to matching edges on right side of A, whipstitch together as indicated. Glue Plume to Back and Hands to Front as shown. Tie raffia into a bow and trim ends; glue bow to Front as shown.
—Designed by Kristine Loffred

COLOR KEY: Stocking

Metallic cord	Need-loft®	CORD AMOUNT
Gold	#01	2 yds. [1.8m]

Worsted-weight	Need-loft®	YARN AMOUNT
Flesh Tone	#56	12 yds. [11m]
Forest	#29	12 yds. [11m]
Pink	#07	6 yds. [5.5m]
Royal	#32	5 yds. [4.6m]
White	#41	4 yds. [3.7m]
Black	#00	3 yds. [2.7m]
Christmas Red	#02	2 yds. [1.8m]
Burgundy	#03	1 yd. [0.9m]
Gray	#38	1 yd. [0.9m]

OTHER:
- Backstitch/Straight
- Brim Attachment
- Nose Attachment
- Beard Attachment

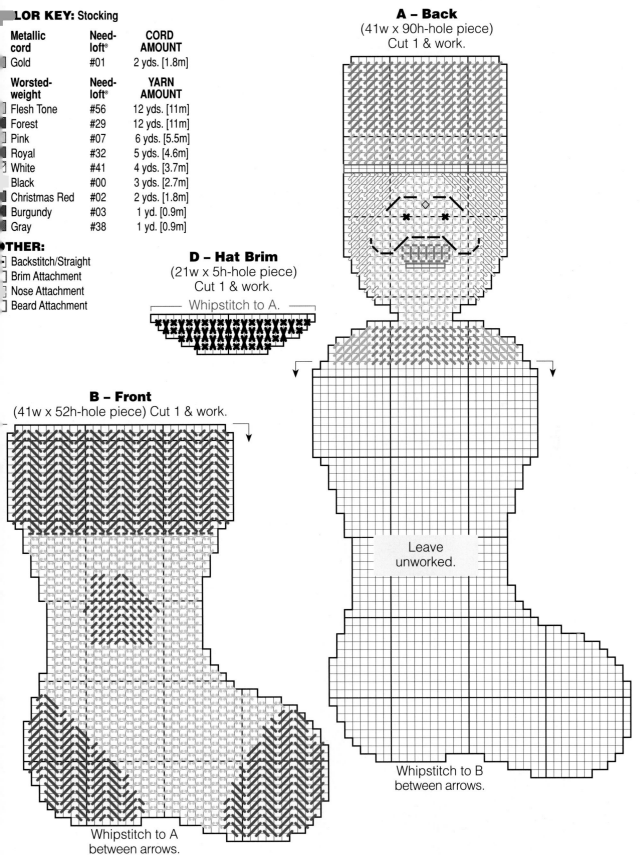

D – Hat Brim
(21w x 5h-hole piece)
Cut 1 & work.
Whipstitch to A.

A – Back
(41w x 90h-hole piece)
Cut 1 & work.

B – Front
(41w x 52h-hole piece) Cut 1 & work.

Leave unworked.

Whipstitch to A between arrows.

Whipstitch to B between arrows.

Match Holder

Cleverly contain those
fireplace matches in this delightful holder.

SIZE: 4⅝" square x 11¾" tall [11.7cm x 29.8cm].

SKILL LEVEL: Easy

MATERIALS:
- Three Sheets of QuickCount® 7-mesh Plastic Canvas by Uniek, Inc.
- Needloft® Craft Cord by Uniek, Inc.; for amount see Color Key.
- Needloft® Yarn by Uniek, Inc. or worsted yarn; for amounts see Color Key.

CUTTING INSTRUCTIONS:
A: For Sides, cut four 26w x 77h-holes.
B: For Bottom, cut one 30w x 30h-holes.

STITCHING INSTRUCTIONS:
1: Using colors indicated and continental stitch, work pieces according to graphs; fill in uncoded areas of A using white and

COLOR KEY: Match Holder

Metallic cord	Needloft®	CORD AMOUNT
☐ Gold	#01	8 yds. [7.3m]

Worsted-weight	Needloft®	YARN AMOUNT
☐ White	#41	60 yds. [54.9m]
■ Black	#00	22 yds. [20.1m]
■ Burgundy	#03	15 yds. [13.7m]
■ Red	#01	14 yds. [12.8m]
■ Royal	#32	12 yds. [11m]
■ Forest	#29	11 yds. [10.1m]
☐ Holly	#27	7 yds. [6.4m]
⊠ Silver	#37	7 yds. [6.4m]
☐ Pink	#07	6 yds. [5.5m]
■ Gray	#38	3 yds. [2.7m]
■ Lavender	#05	2 yds. [1.8m]

OTHER:
- ⊟ Backstitch/Straight
- ☐ Sides/Bottom

ntinental stitch. With black, overcast
dges of B.
Using yarn (Separate into individual
ies, if desired.) and straight stitch,
mbroider mouth on A pieces as indicat-
d on graph.
With white, whipstitch long edges of
pieces wrong sides together; with
lack, whipstitch assembly to right side
f B as indicated. With cord, overcast
nfinished edges.

—Designed by Mike Vickery

B – Bottom
(30w x 30h-hole piece) Cut 1 & work.

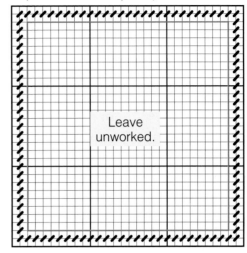

Leave
unworked.

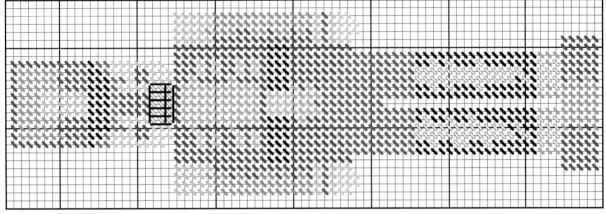

Stocking

structions on page 88

E – Nose
(4w x 4h-hole piece)
Cut 1 & work.

C – Hat Plume
3w x 13h-hole piece)
Cut 1 & work.

F – Beard
(7w x 11h-hole piece)
Cut 1 & work.

Whipstitch to A.

G – Hand #1 & #2
(8w x 6h-hole pieces)
Cut 1 each & work.

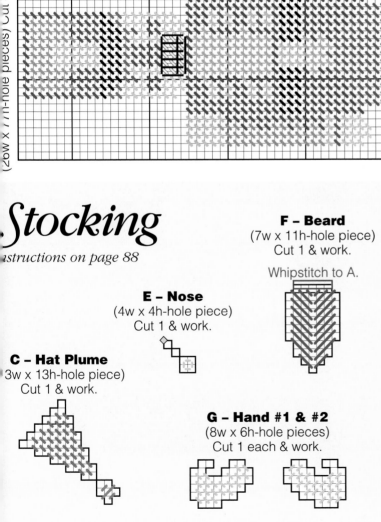

COLOR KEY: Stocking

Metallic cord	Need-loft®	CORD AMOUNT
Gold	#01	2 yds. [1.8m]

Worsted-weight	Need-loft®	YARN AMOUNT
Flesh Tone	#56	12 yds. [11m]
Forest	#29	12 yds. [11m]
Pink	#07	6 yds. [5.5m]
Royal	#32	5 yds. [4.6m]
White	#41	4 yds. [3.7m]
Black	#00	3 yds. [2.7m]
Christmas Red	#02	2 yds. [1.8m]
Burgundy	#03	1 yd. [0.9m]
Gray	#38	1 yd. [0.9m]

OTHER:
- Backstitch/Straight
- Brim Attachment
- Nose Attachment
- Beard Attachment

Frame

Display your seasonal memories in this festive frame.

SIZE: 4½" x 6½" [11.4cm x 16.5cm], not including motif, with a 3⅛" x 5⅛" [7.9cm x 13cm] photo window.

SKILL LEVEL: Average

MATERIALS:
- One Sheet of QuickCount® 7-mesh Plastic Canvas by Uniek, Inc.
- Four green 15mm x 25mm holly leaf sequins
- Two red 8mm round faceted beads
- Craft glue or glue gun
- Needloft® Craft Cord by Uniek, Inc.; for amounts see Color Key.
- Needloft® Yarn by Uniek, Inc. or worsted yarn; for amounts see Color Key.

CUTTING INSTRUCTIONS:
A: For Frame Front, cut one according to graph.
B: For Frame Back, cut one 41w x 27h-holes (no graph).
C: For Frame Stand, cut one according to graph.
D: For Nutcracker Motif, cut one accordin to graph.
E: For Nutcracker Motif Hat Brim, cut one according to graph.
F: For Nutcracker Motif Beard, cut one according to graph.

STITCHING INSTRUCTIONS:
NOTE: B and C pieces are not worked.
1: Using colors and stitches indicated, wor

(Omit stitches within attachment areas.)
...d D-F pieces according to graphs. With
...een cord for cutout and with dk. royal,
...vercast edges of A; omitting attachment
...dges, with matching colors, overcast
...dges of D-F pieces.

...Using cord and yarn (Separate yarn into
...dividual plies, if desired.) in colors and
...mbroidery stitches indicated, embroider
...etail on D as indicated on graph.

...Whipstitch A-C pieces together as
...dicated and according to Frame
...ssembly Diagram. With black, whipstitch

E to right side of D as indicated. Glue
Beard to Nutcracker Motif (see photo).
Glue Nutcracker Motif, holly sequins and
beads to Frame as shown or as desired.

—Designed by Kristine Loffredo

Frame Assembly Diagram
(Pieces are shown in different colors
for contrast; gray denotes wrong side.)

Step 1:
With dk. royal, whipstitch C to center
of B at matching bottom edges.

Step 2:
Holding B to
wrong side of
A, work
remaining
stitches within
attachment
edges
according to
A graph.

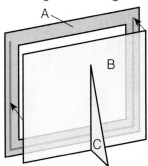

D – Nutracker Motif
(11w x 29h-hole piece)
Cut 1 & work.

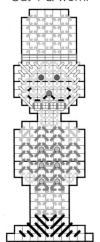

C – Frame Stand
8w x 24h-hole piece)
...t 1 & leave unworked.

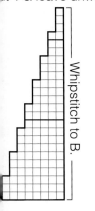

Whipstitch to B.

E – Nutcracker Motif Hat Brim
(7w x 2h-hole piece)
Cut 1 & work.

Whipstitch to D.

F – Nutcracker Motif Beard
(4w x 4h-hole piece)
Cut 1 & work.

Top

A – Frame Front
(43w x 30h-hole piece) Cut 1 & work.

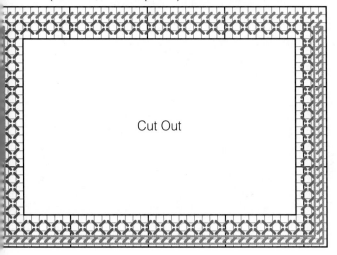

Cut Out

COLOR KEY: Frame

Metallic cord	Need-loft®	CORD AMOUNT
Green	#04	4 yds. [3.7m]
Gold	#01	2 yds. [1.8m]

Worsted-weight	Need-loft®	YARN AMOUNT
Dark Royal	#48	6 yds. [5.5m]
Black	#00	1 yd. [0.9m]
Orchid	#44	1 yd. [0.9m]
Red	#01	1 yd. [0.9m]
Royal	#32	1 yd. [0.9m]
White	#41	1 yd. [0.9m]
Cinnamon	#14	1/4 yd. [0.2m]

OTHER:
- Backstitch/Straight
- French Knot
- Hat Brim Attachment
- Frame Front/Back Attachment

Tote

Make your holiday shopping easier with this handy Tote.

ZE: 3⅞" x 7⅜" x 9¾" tall [9.8cm x 18.7cm 24.8cm], not including handles.

KILL LEVEL: Easy

ATERIALS:
Three Sheets of QuickCount® 7-mesh
Plastic Canvas by Uniek, Inc.
⅔ yd. [0.6m] burgundy ½" [13mm]
decorative braid or twisted cording
Craft glue or glue gun
Needloft® Yarn by Uniek, Inc. or worsted
yarn; for amounts see Color Key.

UTTING INSTRUCTIONS:
: For Sides, cut two according to graph.
: For Ends, cut two 25w x 65h-holes
o graph).
: For Bottom, cut one 49w x 25h-holes
o graph).

STITCHING INSTRUCTIONS:
NOTE: C is not worked.
1: Using colors and stitches indicated, work A according to graph; work B according to pattern established on A. With matching colors, overcast cutout edges of A pieces.
2: With dk. royal, whipstitch A-C pieces together, forming Tote; overcast unfinished top edges.
NOTE: Cut decorative braid or cording in half.
3: For each handle, thread one end of one braid or cording length from outside to inside through each cutout on one A; glue ends on inside to secure.

—*Designed by Michele Wilcox*

COLOR KEY: Tote

Worsted-weight	Need-loft®	YARN AMOUNT
■ Dark Royal	#48	90 yds. [82.3m]
■ Beige	#40	80 yds. [73.2m]

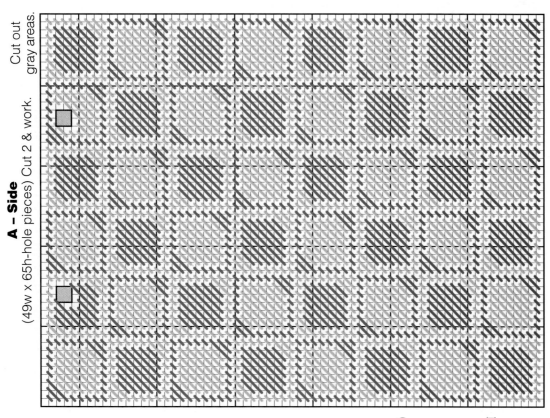

Cut out gray areas.

A – Side
(49w x 65h-hole pieces) Cut 2 & work.

Soldier Doorstop

Add an extra seasonal
touch with this sitting Soldier Doorstop.

SIZE: 2½" x 13" x 11¼" tall [6.4cm x 33cm x 28.6cm].

SKILL LEVEL: Average

MATERIALS:
- Two Sheets of QuickCount® 7-mesh Plastic Canvas by Uniek, Inc.
- 1 yd. [0.9m] natural raffia
- Zip-close bag filled with gravel or other weighting material
- Craft glue or glue gun
- Needloft® Craft Cord by Uniek, Inc.; for amounts see Color Key.
- Needloft® Yarn by Uniek, Inc. or worste yarn; for amounts see Color Key.

CUTTING INSTRUCTIONS:
NOTE: Graphs continued on page 100.
A: For Back, cut one according to graph.

: For Front, cut one 56w x 27h-holes.
: For Sides, cut two 16w x 27h-holes.
: For Top & Bottom, cut two (one for
op and one for Bottom) 56w x 16h-holes.
: For Hat Plume, cut one according
 graph.
: For Hat Brim, cut one according
 graph.
: For Nose, cut one according to graph.
: For Beard, cut one according to graph.
 For Hands #1 and #2, cut one each
cording to graphs.
 For House, cut one according to graph.

TITCHING INSTRUCTIONS:

: Using colors and stitches indicated,
ork pieces according to graphs. Omitting
tachment edges, with matching colors,
ercast edges of A and E-J pieces.
: Using cord and yarn (Separate into
dividual plies, if desired.) in colors and
mbroidery stitches indicated, embroider
etail on A as indicated on graph.
: With black, whipstitch F to right side
 A as indicated. With matching colors,
hipstitch B-D pieces wrong sides
gether; whipstitch assembly to right side
 A as indicated, inserting weighting
aterial before closing.

NOTE: Cut raffia into six 6" [15.2cm] lengths.
4: Holding raffia lengths together, tie a knot
in center; trim and fray ends as desired
(see photo). Glue raffia knot to Front and
House over raffia knot as shown in photo.
Glue Plume, Nose and Beard to Back
as shown.

—*Designed by Kristine Loffredo*

COLOR KEY: Soldier Doorstop

Metallic cord	Need-loft®	CORD AMOUNT
■ Red/Black	#45	6 yds. [5.5m]
■ Gold	#01	4 yds. [3.7m]

Worsted-weight	Need-loft®	YARN AMOUNT
▨ Flesh Tone	#56	37 yds. [33.8m]
■ Royal	#32	10 yds. [9.1m]
■ Forest	#29	6 yds. [5.5m]
▨ Orchid	#44	6 yds. [5.5m]
■ Black	#00	5 yds. [4.6m]
▧ White	#41	5 yds. [4.6m]
■ Burgundy	#03	3 yds. [2.7m]
■ Red	#01	3 yds. [2.7m]
▨ Gray	#38	1 yd. [0.9m]

OTHER:
⊟ Backstitch/Straight
⊙ French Knot
☐ Back/Hat Brim Attachment
☐ Front/Cover Attachment

C – Side
(16w x 27h-hole pieces)
Cut 2 & work.

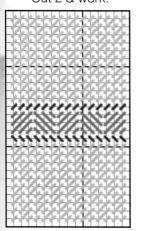

B – Front
(56w x 27h-hole piece) Cut 1 & work.

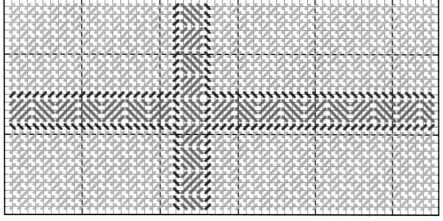

COLOR KEY: Soldier Doorstop

Metallic cord	Need-loft®	CORD AMOUNT
■ Red/Black	#45	6 yds. [5.5m]
■ Gold	#01	4 yds. [3.7m]

Worsted-weight	Need-loft®	YARN AMOUNT
■ Flesh Tone	#56	37 yds. [33.8m]
■ Royal	#32	10 yds. [9.1m]
■ Forest	#29	6 yds. [5.5m]
■ Orchid	#44	6 yds. [5.5m]
■ Black	#00	5 yds. [4.6m]
◻ White	#41	5 yds. [4.6m]
■ Burgundy	#03	3 yds. [2.7m]
■ Red	#01	3 yds. [2.7m]
■ Gray	#38	1 yd. [0.9m]

OTHER:
- ▬ Backstitch/Straight
- ● French Knot
- ◻ Back/Hat Brim Attachment
- ◻ Front/Cover Attachment

G – Nose
(4w x 9h-hole piece)
Cut 1 & work.

I – Hand #1 & #2
(6w x 9h-hole pieces)
Cut 1 each & work.

H – Beard
(10w x 14h-hole piece)
Cut 1 & work.

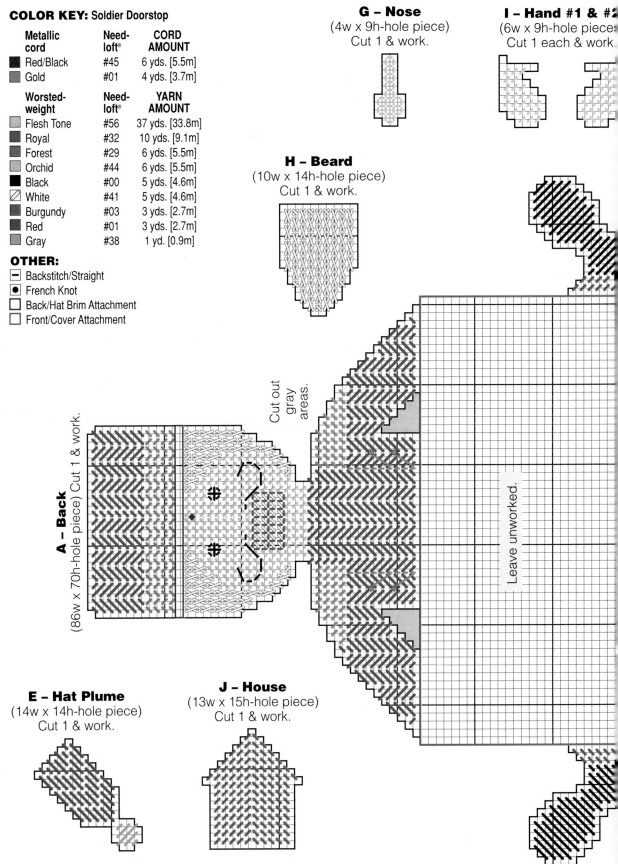

Cut out gray areas.

A – Back
(86w x 70h-hole piece) Cut 1 & work.

Leave unworked.

E – Hat Plume
(14w x 14h-hole piece)
Cut 1 & work.

J – House
(13w x 15h-hole piece)
Cut 1 & work.

Tissue Cover

*You'll replace sniffles with smiles
when you bring out this country style Tissue Cover.*

SIZE: Loosely covers a boutique-style tissue box.

SKILL LEVEL: Easy

MATERIALS:
Two Sheets of 7-mesh plastic canvas
Velcro® closure (optional)
Six-strand embroidery floss; for amount see Color Key.
Worsted-weight or plastic canvas yarn; for amounts see Color Key.

CUTTING INSTRUCTIONS:
For Top, cut one according graph.
For Sides, cut four 31w x h-holes.
For Optional Bottom and Flap, cut one 31w x 31h-holes for bottom and one 31w x 12h-holes for Flap (no graphs).

STITCHING INSTRUCTIONS:
NOTE: C pieces are not worked.
Using colors and stitches indicated, work A and B pieces according to graphs. With dk. sage, overcast cutout edges of A.
Using six strands red floss and

backstitch, embroider detail on A and B pieces as indicated on graphs.
3: With dk. sage, whipstitch A and B pieces together, forming Cover; overcast unfinished bottom edges. For Optional Bottom, before overcasting, whipstitch C pieces together and to one Cover side according to Optional Tissue Cover Bottom Assembly Illustration. Glue closure to Flap and inside Cover (see illustration).

—Designed by Debbie Tabor

**Optional Tissue
Cover Bottom
Assembly Illustration**

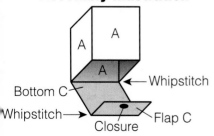

B – Side
(31w x 35h-hole pieces) Cut 4 & work.

COLOR KEY: Tissue Cover

Embroidery floss	AMOUNT
■ Red	29 yds. [26.5m]

Worsted-weight	YARN AMOUNT
■ Dk. Sage	42 yds. [38.4m]
▨ Eggshell	40 yds. [36.6m]
■ Lt. Sage	20 yds. [18.3m]
■ Country Red	4 yds. [3.7m]

STITCH KEY:
⊟ Backstitch/Straight

A – Top
(31w x 31h-hole piece) Cut 1 & work.

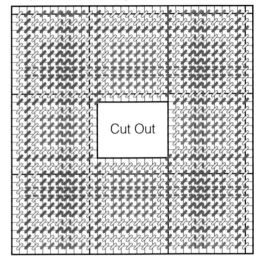

Cut Out

Soldier Doorstop

Instructions on page 96

F – Hat Brim
(24w x 5h-hole piece) Cut 1 & work.

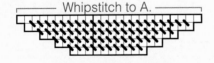

Whipstitch to A.

D – Top & Bottom
(56w x 16h-hole pieces) Cut 2. Work 1 for Top & 1 for Bottom.

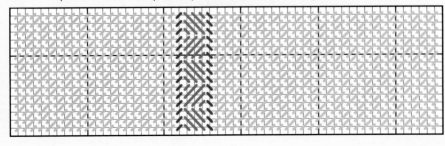

COLOR KEY: Soldier Doorstop

Metallic cord	Need-loft®	CORD AMOUN
■ Red/Black	#45	6 yds. [5.
□ Gold	#01	4 yds. [3.

Worsted-weight	Need-loft®	YARN AMOUN
□ Flesh Tone	#56	37 yds. [33
■ Royal	#32	10 yds. [9.
■ Forest	#29	6 yds. [5.
□ Orchid	#44	6 yds. [5.
■ Black	#00	5 yds. [4.
▨ White	#41	5 yds. [4.
■ Burgundy	#03	3 yds. [2.
■ Red	#01	3 yds. [2.
■ Gray	#38	1 yd. [0.9

OTHER:
⊟ Backstitch/Straight
● French Knot
☐ Back/Hat Brim Attachment
☐ Front/Cover Attachment

CHAPTER FIVE

Frosty Friends

Create your own winter wonderland
with projects that are sure to warm
your heart. This adorable
assortment of polar pals will
brighten a wintry day.
Whether you make them to
keep or give as gifts, your
family and friends will
be delighted with these
Frosty Friends.

Card Guard

*This wintry friend is dressed for the
season and will cheerfully display your special greetings.*

SIZE: 4" x 7½" x 8¾" tall [10.2cm x 19.1cm
x 22.2cm].

SKILL LEVEL: Average

MATERIALS:
- Two Sheets of QuickCount® 7-mesh
  Plastic Canvas by Uniek, Inc.
- Six 5mm pearl beads
- Sewing needle and white thread
- Craft glue or glue gun
- No. 3 Pearl Cotton (Coton Perlé) Art. 117
  by DMC® or six-strand embroidery floss;

for amounts see Color Key.
- Needloft® Yarn by Uniek, Inc. or worste
  yarn; for amounts see Color Key.

CUTTING INSTRUCTIONS:
A: For Front, cut one according to graph.
B: For Back, cut one 49w x 33h-holes
(no graph).
C: For Sides, cut two 25w x 33h-holes
(no graph).
D: For Bottom, cut one 49w x 25h-holes
(no graph).

STITCHING INSTRUCTIONS:

1: Using colors and stitches indicated, work A according to graph; work B and C pieces according to Back & Side Stitch Pattern Guide, and D according to Bottom Stitch Pattern Guide.

2: Using pearl cotton or six strands floss and embroidery stitches indicated, embroider detail on A-C pieces as indicated on graph and Back & Side Stitch Pattern Guide.

3: With thread, sew pearl beads to A as indicated. With royal, whipstitch pieces together according to Card Guard Assembly Illustration; with matching colors, overcast unfinished edges.

—Designed by Michele Wilcox

Bottom Stitch Pattern Guide

Continue established pattern up & across entire piece.

Back & Side Stitch Pattern Guide

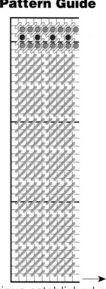

Continue established pattern across each entire piece.

Card Guard Assembly Illustration

(Pieces are shown in different colors for contrast; gray denotes wrong side.)

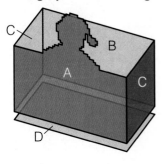

COLOR KEY: Card Guard

Pearl cotton or floss	DMC®	AMOUNT
Vy. Lt. Topaz	#727	7 yds. [6.4m]
Kelly Green	#702	4 yds. [3.7m]
Black	#310	3 yds. [2.7m]
Sky Blue	#519	1 yd. [0.9m]

Worsted-weight	Need-loft®	YARN AMOUNT
Royal	#32	80 yds. [73.2m]
White	#41	25 yds. [22.9m]
Red	#01	12 yds. [11m]
Christmas Green	#28	1 yd. [0.9m]
Yellow	#57	1 yd. [0.9m]

OTHER:
- Backstitch/Straight
- French Knot
- Lazy Daisy
- Bead Attachment

A – Front
(49w x 57h-hole piece) Cut 1 & work.

Heart-Warmer

Welcome winter inside with
this heartwarming wall hanging.

ZE: 10¼" x about 16" [26cm x 40.6cm].

KILL LEVEL: Easy

ATERIALS:
1½ Sheets of QuickCount® 7-mesh Plastic Canvas by Uniek, Inc.
Four red 3mm beads
Four red ½" [13mm] sew-on buttons
Sewing needle and red and white thread
One 9" x 12" [22.9cm x 30.5cm] Sheet of White QuickStick® Adhesive Felt Rectangle by CPE
Red crayon
Craft glue or glue gun
No. 5 Pearl Cotton (Coton Perlé) Art. 116 by DMC® or six-strand embroidery floss; for amounts see Color Key.
Needloft® Yarn by Uniek, Inc. or worsted yarn; for amounts see Color Key.

UTTING INSTRUCTIONS:
: For Child, cut one according to graph.
: For Snowman, cut one according graph.
: For Sign, cut one according to graph.

TITCHING INSTRUCTIONS:
: Using colors and stitches indicated,

work A and C pieces according to graphs; using white and continental stitch, work B. With white for sign and with matching colors, overcast edges of pieces.
2: Using pearl cotton or three strands floss and embroidery stitches indicated, embroider detail on pieces as indicated on graphs.
3: Using white thread for beads and red thread for buttons, sew embellishments to A and B pieces as indicated.
4: With crayon, lightly stroke color on

COLOR KEY: Heart-Warmer

Pearl cotton or floss	DMC®	AMOUNT
■ Black	#310	5 yds. [4.6m]
■ Red	#321	5 yds. [4.6m]

Worsted-weight	Need-loft®	YARN AMOUNT
▨ White	#41	45 yds. [41.1m]
■ Holly	#27	20 yds. [18.3m]
■ Tangerine	#11	10 yds. [9.1m]
■ Royal	#32	9 yds. [8.2m]
■ Red	#01	6 yds. [5.5m]
■ Maple	#13	5 yds. [4.6m]
▨ Sandstone	#16	3 yds. [2.7m]

OTHER:
⊟ Backstitch/Straight
⬤ French Knot
◙ Button Attachment
◎ Bead Attachment

A – Child
(43w x 69h-hole piece)
Cut 1 & work.

Child's cheeks (see photo). Glue Child and Snowman together and to right side of Sign as shown.

NOTE: For backing, using assembly as pattern, cut felt ⅛" [3mm] smaller at all edges.

5: Following manufacturer's instructions, attach backing to wrong side of assembly. Hang or display as desired.

—Designed by Michele Wilcox

B – Snowman
(37w x 56h-hole piece)
Cut 1 & work.

COLOR KEY: Heart-Warmer

Pearl cotton or floss	DMC®	AMOUNT
■ Black	#310	5 yds. [4.6m]
■ Red	#321	5 yds. [4.6m]

Worsted-weight	Need-loft®	YARN AMOUNT
▱ White	#41	45 yds. [41.1m]
■ Holly	#27	20 yds. [18.3m]
■ Tangerine	#11	10 yds. [9.1m]
■ Royal	#32	9 yds. [8.2m]
■ Red	#01	6 yds. [5.5m]
■ Maple	#13	5 yds. [4.6m]
■ Sandstone	#16	3 yds. [2.7m]

OTHER:
- ⊟ Backstitch/Straight
- ⚫ French Knot
- ⊡ Button Attachment
- ⊡ Bead Attachment

C – Sign
(61w x 45h-hole piece) Cut 1 & work.

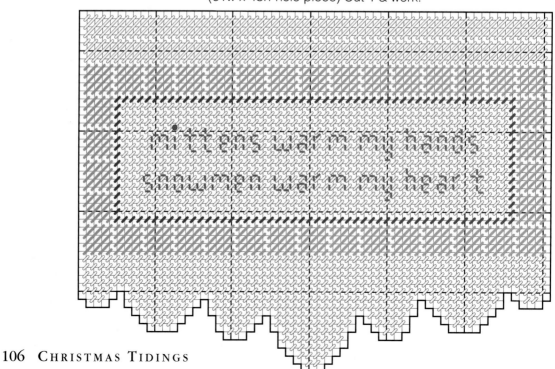

Tic-Tac Snowman

*Young and old alike will enjoy a
winter afternoon indoors with this frosty friend.*

SIZE: 10½" x 13½" [26.7cm x 34.3cm].

SKILL LEVEL: Easy

MATERIALS:
- Two sheets of 7-mesh plastic canvas
- Worsted-weight or plastic canvas yarn; for amounts see Color Key.

CUTTING INSTRUCTIONS:
A: For Snowman, cut one according to graph.
B: For Bow Tie, cut one according to graph.
C: For Snowball Game Pieces, cut five according to graph.
D: For Snowflake Game Pieces, cut five according to graph.

STITCHING INSTRUCTIONS:
1: Using colors and stitches indicated, wor
pieces according to graphs; with red for
Snowman's hat as shown in photo and
with gray, overcast edges of pieces.
2: Glue Bow Tie to right side of Snowmar
as shown in photo.

—Designed by Terry Ricic

B – Bow Tie
(19w x 8h-hole piece)
Cut 1 & work.

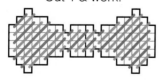

C – Snowball Game Piece
(12w x 12h-hole pieces)
Cut 5 & work.

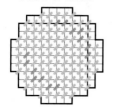

D – Snowflake Game Piece
(13w x 15h-hole pieces)
Cut 5 & work.

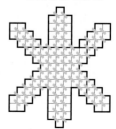

OLOR KEY: Tic Tac Snowman

Worsted-weight	YARN AMOUNT
White	70 yds. [64m]
Gray	30 yds. [27.4m]
Red	9 yds. [8.2m]
Black	2 yds. [1.8m]

A – Snowman
(70w x 90h-hole piece)
Cut 1 & work.

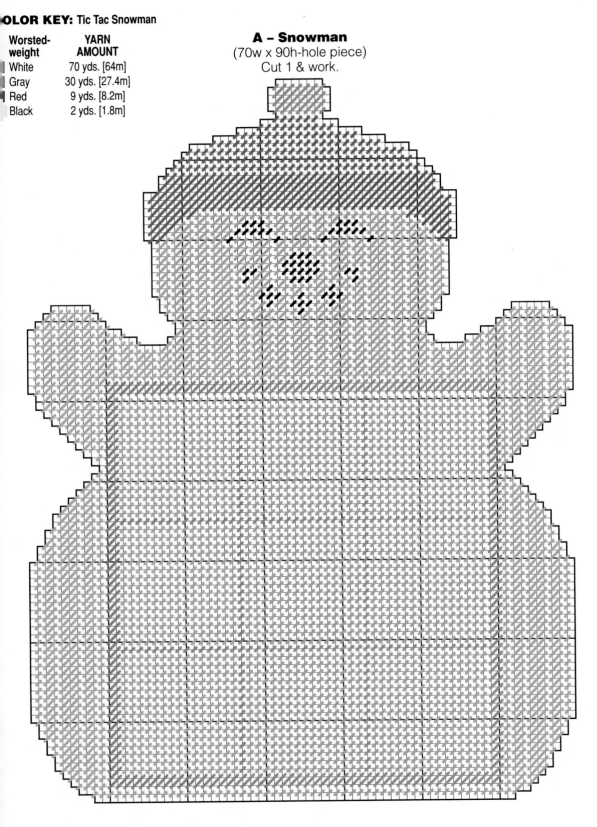

Belly Bumpers

Bring a touch of winter
fun inside with these polar pals.

SIZES: Snowman and Penguin are 5" x 7¼"
[12.7cm x 18.4cm]; Polar Bear is 6¼" x 8¼"
[15.9cm x 21cm].

SKILL LEVEL: Average

MATERIALS:
Two Sheets of Clear, One Sheet Each of
Black and White and ½ Sheet of Forest
QuickCount® 7-mesh Plastic Canvas by
Uniek, Inc.
Six brown/black 4mm animal eyes
One red ½" [13mm] pom-pom
Craft glue or glue gun
Needloft® Craft Cord by Uniek, Inc.; for
amounts see individual Color Keys.
Six-strand embroidery floss; for amounts
see individual Color Keys.
Needloft® Yarn by Uniek, Inc. or worsted
yarn; for amounts see individual
Color Keys.

SNOWMAN
CUTTING INSTRUCTIONS:
A: For Snowman Back and Backing, cut
two (one from clear for Back and one from
white for Backing) according to graph.
B: For Snowman Middle and Backing, cut
two (one from clear for Middle and one
from white for Backing) according to graph.
C: For Snowman Head and Backing, cut
two (one from clear for Head and one from
white for Backing) according to graph.
D: For Hat and Backing, cut two (one from
clear for Hat and one from forest for
Backing) according to graph.

STITCHING INSTRUCTIONS:
1: Using colors and stitches indicated, work
pieces according to graphs. Using six
strands floss in colors and embroidery

stitches indicated, embroider detail on C
and D pieces as indicated on graphs.
2: For Back, Middle and Head (make 1
each), holding Backing to wrong side of
corresponding worked piece, with cord
(see photo) and with matching colors,
whipstitch together. For Hat, holding Backing
D to wrong side of Hat D, with forest,
whipstitch together as indicated; with forest,
overcast unfinished edges of Hat D.
3: Glue Head inside Hat (see photo); glue
Hat to Middle and Middle to Back as
shown in photo. Glue eyes to Head C as
indicated. Display as desired.

PENGUIN
STITCHING INSTRUCTIONS:
A: For Penguin Back and Backing, cut two
(one from clear for Back and one from
black for Backing) according to graph.
B: For Penguin Middle and Backing, cut
two (one from clear for Middle and one
from black for Backing) according to graph.
C: For Penguin Head and Backing, cut two
(one from clear for Head and one from
black for Backing) according to graph.
D: For Hat and Backing, cut two (one from
clear for Hat and one from white for
Backing) according to graph.

STITCHING INSTRUCTIONS:
1: Using colors and stitches indicated, work
pieces according to graphs. Using six
strands floss and French knot, embroider
detail on C as indicated on graph.
2: For Back, Middle and Head (make 1
each), holding Backing to wrong side of
corresponding worked piece, with cord
(see photo) and with matching colors,
whipstitch together. For Hat, holding
Backing D to wrong side of Hat D, with

matching colors, whipstitch together; with Christmas red, overcast unfinished edges of Hat D.

3: Glue Head inside Hat (see photo); glue pom-pom to Hat and Hat to Middle; glue Middle to Back as shown in photo. Glue eyes to Head C as indicated. Display as desired.

POLAR BEAR

CUTTING INSTRUCTIONS:

A: For Polar Bear Back and Backing, cut two (one from clear for Back and one from white for Backing) according to graph.
B: For Polar Bear Middle and Backing, cut two (one from clear for Middle and one from white for Backing) according to graph.
C: For Polar Bear Head and Backing, cut two (one from clear for Head and one from white for Backing) according to graph.

STITCHING INSTRUCTIONS:

1: Using colors and stitches indicated, work pieces according to graphs. Using six strands floss and embroidery stitches indicated, embroider detail on pieces as indicated on graphs.

2: For Back, Middle and Head (make 1 each), holding Backing to wrong side of corresponding worked piece, with cord (see photo) and with matching colors, whipstitch together.

3: Glue eyes to Head; glue Head to Middle and Middle to Back as shown in photo. Display as desired.

—*Designed by Dawn Aust*

C – Polar Bear Head & Backing
(16w x 26h-hole pieces)
Cut 1 from clear for Head & work; cut 1 from white for Backing & leave unworked.

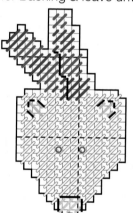

A – Polar Bear Back & Backing
(54w x 26h-hole pieces)
Cut 1 from clear for Front & work; cut 1 from white for Backing & leave unworked.

COLOR KEY: Polar Bear

Metallic cord	Need-loft®	CORD AMOUN
☐ Blue	#49	8 yds. [7.
Embroidery floss		AMOUN
■ Black		4 yds. [3.
Worsted-weight	**Need-loft®**	**YARN AMOUN**
▨ White	#41	20 yds. [18
■ Holly	#27	2 yds. [1.
▦ Pink	#07	2 yds. [1.
■ Royal	#32	2 yds. [1.
▨ Black	#00	1/4 yd. [0.

OTHER:
- ⊟ Backstitch/Straight
- ⊚ Eye Placement

B – Polar Bear Middle & Backing
(42w x 21h-hole pieces)
Cut 1 from clear for Middle & work; cut 1
from white for Backing & leave unworked.

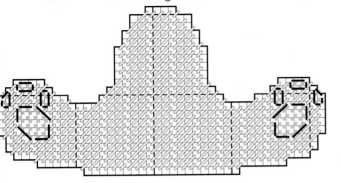

C – Penguin Head & Backing
(14w x 12h-hole pieces)
Cut 1 from clear for Head & work; cut 1
from black for Backing & leave unworked.

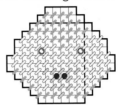

A – Penguin Back & Backing
(48w x 25h-hole pieces)
Cut 1 from clear for Back & work; cut 1
from black for Backing & leave unworked.

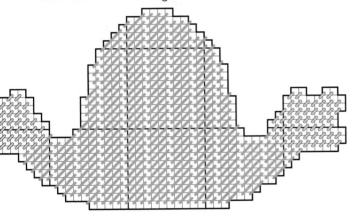

COLOR KEY: Penguin

Metallic cord	Need-loft®	CORD AMOUNT
☐ Black	#44	7 yds. [6.4m]

Embroidery floss		AMOUNT
■ Black		1/4 yd. [0.2m]

Worsted-weight	Need-loft®	YARN AMOUNT
▨ Black	#00	13 yds. [11.9m]
▨ Yellow	#57	4 yds. [3.7m]
▨ White	#41	3 yds. [2.7m]
■ Christmas Red	#02	1 yd. [0.9m]

OTHER:
● French Knot
◎ Eye Placement

B – Penguin Middle & Backing
(40w x 19h-hole pieces)
Cut 1 from clear for Middle & work; cut 1
from black for Backing & leave unworked.

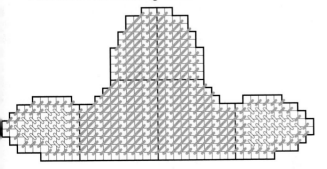

D – Penguin Hat & Backing
(12w x 7h-hole pieces)
Cut 1 from clear for Hat & work; cut 1
from white for Backing & leave unworked.

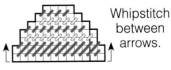

Whipstitch
between
arrows.

D – Snowman Hat & Backing

(24w x 84h-hole pieces)
Cut 1 from clear & work for Hat; cut 1 from
forest & leave unworked for Backing.

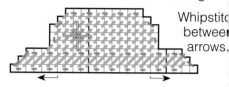

Whipstitc
betwee
arrows.

A – Snowman Back & Backing

(48w x 25h-hole pieces)
Cut 1 from clear for Back & work; cut 1
from white for Backing & leave unworked.

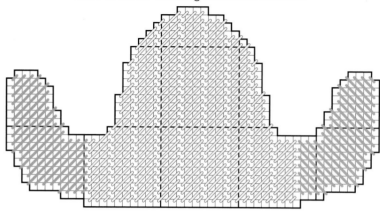

COLOR KEY: Snowman

Pearlized cord	Need-loft®	CORD AMOUNT
☐ White	#33	4 yds. [3.7m]

Embroidery floss		AMOUNT
■ Black		4 yds. [3.7m]
▨ Burgundy		1 yd. [0.9m]
▨ Gold Metallic		1 yd. [0.9m]

Worsted-weight	Need-loft®	YARN AMOUNT
▨ White	#41	14 yds. [12.8m]
▨ Forest	#29	7 yds. [6.4m]
▨ Burgundy	#03	4 yds. [3.7m]
▨ Bright Orange	#58	1/4 yd. [0.2m]

OTHER:
- ⊟ Backstitch/Straight
- ⦿ French Knot
- ⊡ Eye Placement

B – Snowman Middle & Backing

(44w x 20h-hole pieces)
Cut 1 from clear for Middle & work; cut 1
from white for Backing & leave unworked.

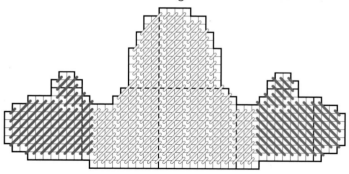

C – Snowman Head & Backing

(11w x 11h-hole pieces)
Cut 1 from clear for Head & work; cut 1 from
white for Backing & leave unworked.

Perky Penguin

*This Perky Penguin reminds us of the
outdoor fun we can have during the winter season.*

SIZE: 4" x 8½" x 13" tall [10.2cm x 1.3cm x 33cm].

SKILL LEVEL: Challenging

MATERIALS:
- Two Sheets of QuickCount® 7-mesh Plastic Canvas by Uniek, Inc.
- 10" [25.4cm] length of ¼" [6mm] wooden dowel
- One wooden 1¾" [4.4cm] wheel
- White craft paint and paint brush
- Zip-close sandwich bag filled with gravel or other weighting material
- Craft glue or glue gun
- ⅛" [3mm] Metallic Ribbon by Kreinik or metallic cord; for amount see Color Key.
- No. 3 Pearl Cotton (Coton Perlé) Art. 115 by DMC® or six-strand embroidery floss; for amount see Color Key.
- America's Best Rayon Crochet Thread Art. 137 by Elmore-Pisgah, Inc. or chenille yarn; for amounts see Color Key.
- Needloft® Yarn by Uniek, Inc. or worsted yarn; for amounts see individual Color Keys.

CUTTING INSTRUCTIONS:
A: For Penguin, cut one according to graph.
B: For Base Top & Bottom, cut two (one for Top and one for Bottom) according to graph.
C: For Base Side Pieces, cut two 44w x 8h-holes.
D: For Dowel Sleeve, cut one 6w x 10h-holes (no graph).

STITCHING INSTRUCTIONS:
NOTES: D is not worked.
Use a doubled strand of crochet thread or chenille yarn throughout.

1: Using colors and stitches indicated, work A-C pieces according to graphs; fill in uncoded areas of A using white plastic canvas or worsted yarn and continental stitch. Omitting scarf edges, with matching colors, overcast edges of A.
2: Using plastic canvas or worsted yarn (Separate into individual plies, if desired.) and pearl cotton or six strands floss in colors and embroidery stitches indicated, embroider detail on A as indicated on graph.
NOTE: Cut nineteen 2" [5.1cm] lengths of white plastic canvas yarn.
3: For scarf fringe, attach one strand with Lark's Head Knot to each ◆ hole on A as indicated; trim ends to even. With white worsted yarn, whipstitch D to wrong side of A as indicated.
NOTE: Paint dowel and wheel; let dry.
4: With black plastic canvas or worsted yarn, whipstitch and assemble wheel, dowel, B and C pieces according to Base Assembly Diagram. Slip dowel through Dowel Sleeve, resting bottom of Penguin on Base (see photo).

—Designed by
Janelle Giese of Janelle Marie Designs

COLOR KEY: Perky Penguin

⅛" ribbon	Kreinik	AMOUNT
☐ Silver	#001	5 yds. [4.6m]

Pearl cotton or floss	DMC®	AMOUNT
■ Black	#310	4 yds. [3.7m]

Chenille yarn	Elmore-Pisgah	YARN AMOUNT
■ Cityscape	#117	34 yds. [31.1m]
▨ White	#1	5 yds. [4.6m]

Worsted-weight	Need-loft®	YARN AMOUNT
■ White	#41	20 yds. [18.3m]
■ Black	#00	18 yds. [16.5m]
■ Red	#01	12 yds. [11m]
▨ Yellow	#57	7 yds. [6.4m]
■ Baby Blue	#36	2 yds. [1.8m]
■ Turquoise	#54	1 yd. [0.9m]
■ Burgundy	#03	¼ yd. [0.2m]

OTHER:
☐ Backstitch/Straight
☐ Dowel Sleeve Attachment

C – Base Side Piece
(44w x 8h-hole pieces) Cut 2 & work.

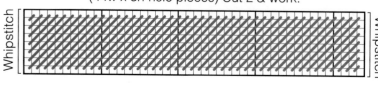

Base Assembly Diagram

Step 1:
Whipstitch short edges of C pieces wrong sides together; Whipstitch one long edge of C pieces to base bottom B.

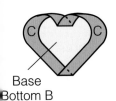

Base Bottom B

Step 2:
Run a line of glue around one dowel end; *insert dowel end into center cutout of wheel.*

—Dowel

Glue
—Wheel

Step 3:
Push opposite dowel end through cutout on base top B; *glue wheel to wrong side of base top B to secure.*

Base Top B
—Dowel

Wheel—

Step 4:
Whipstitch base top B to remaining long edge of C pieces, filling with weighting material before closing.

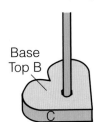

Base Top B

C

A – Penguin
(57w x 75h-hole piece)
Cut 1 & work.

B – Base Top & Bottom
(29w x 25h-hole pieces)
Cut 1 for Top & work; cut 1 for Bottom & leave unworked.

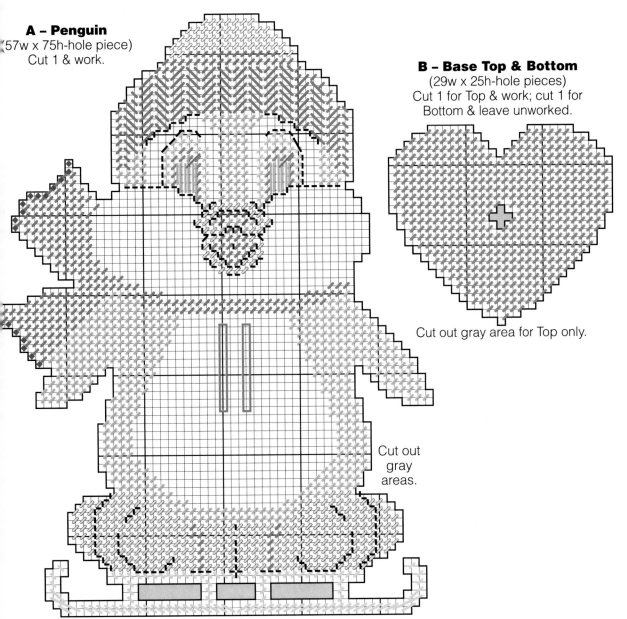

Cut out gray area for Top only.

Cut out gray areas.

Winter Welcome

Celebrate the season with
this Winter Welcome door hanger.

SIZE: 5" x 40" [12.7cm x 101.6cm].

SKILL LEVEL: Challenging

MATERIALS:
- Two sheets of 7-mesh plastic canvas
- Two 6" [15.2cm] QuickShape™ Hexagon Shapes by Uniek, Inc.

COLOR KEY: Winter Welcome

Metallic cord	Need-loft®	CORD AMOUNT
Solid Silver	#21	3 yds. [2.7m]
Gold Frizette	#34	2 yds. [1.8m]

Pearlized cord	Need-loft®	CORD AMOUNT
White Iridescent	#33	5 yds. [4.6m]

Metallic thread	Kreinik	AMOUNT
Solid Pearl	#3200	6 yds. [5.5m]

Satin ribbon		AMOUNT
White		1/4 yd. [0.2m]

Pearl cotton or floss	DMC®	AMOUNT
Black	#310	1 yd. [0.9m]

Worsted-weight	Nylon Plus®	YARN AMOUNT
Aqua Light	#39	30 yds. [27.4m]

Worsted-weight	Need-loft®	YARN AMOUNT
White	#41	10 yds. [9.1m]
Fern	#23	5 yds. [4.6m]
Maple	#13	5 yds. [4.6m]
Red	#01	5 yds. [4.6m]
Royal	#32	4 yds. [3.7m]
Christmas Red	#02	3 yds. [2.7m]
Black	#00	2 yds. [1.8m]
Christmas Green	#28	2 yds. [1.8m]
Cinnamon	#14	1 yd. [0.9m]
Purple	#46	1 yd. [0.9m]
Tangerine	#11	1 yd. [0.9m]
Yellow	#57	1 yd. [0.9m]

STITCH KEY:
- ⊟ Backstitch/Straight
- ● French Knot
- ⊠ Modified Turkey Work

- 1¼ yds. [1m] of white 2¼" [5.7cm] grosgrain ribbon
- White craft paint and paint brush
- One gold ¼" [6mm] jingle bell
- One gold star, six gold ¼" [6mm] round and six red ⅛" [3mm] round sequins
- Fabric Snow-Tex™ Textural Medium by DecoArt™
- White iridescent fine glitter
- Small paint brush
- Aleene's™ Thick Designer Tacky Glue or craft glue and glue gun
- Needloft® Craft Cord by Uniek, Inc.; for amounts see Color Key.
- Ombre Metallic Thread by Kreinik or metallic cord; for amount see Color Key.
- ⅛" [3mm] satin ribbon; for amount see Color Key.
- No. 3 Pearl Cotton (Coton Perlé) Art. 11⁴ by DMC® or six-strand embroidery floss; for amount see Color Key.
- Nylon Plus™ Yarn by Darice or worsted yarn; for amount see Color Key.

B – Letter "W"
(33w x 30h-hole piece)
Cut 1 & work.

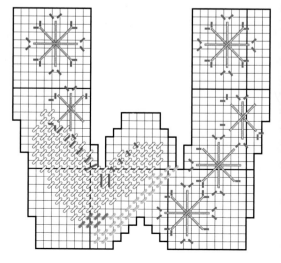

Needloft® Yarn by Uniek, Inc. or worsted
yarn; for amounts see Color Keys.

UTTING INSTRUCTIONS:

: For Snowflakes, cut one from each
exagon shape according to graph.
For Letter "W", cut one according
graph.
For Letter "I", cut one according to graph.
: For Letter "N", cut one according
graph.
For Letter "T", cut one according
graph.
For Letter "E", cut one according to graph.
: For Letter "R", cut one according
graph.

TITCHING INSTRUCTIONS:

OTE: A is not worked.

Using colors and stitches indicated, work
-G according to graphs, filling in uncoded
eas using aqua light and continental
itch. With aqua light, overcast edges of
-G pieces.

: Using yarn (Separate into individual
ies, if desired.), pearlized cord, metallic
read, pearl cotton or six strands floss,
tin ribbon and embroidery stitches
dicated, embroider detail on B, C (Leave
" [13mm] loops on modified turkey work;
o not cut through loops.) and E-G pieces
; indicated on graphs.

OTE: Cut one 9" [22.9cm] length each of
d and Christmas red.

: For package bow, tie red strand into a
ow and trim ends; glue to D as shown in
hoto. Glue jingle bell, star and round
equins to D as shown.

: For sled rope, thread one end of
hristmas red strand through each ◆ hole
n F as indicated; allowing strand to hang
osely at front (see photo); glue ends to
rong side to secure. Using brush and
extured medium, paint A pieces and
rinkle with glitter; let dry.

: Fold under one end of grosgrain ribbon

1½" [3.8cm]; trim opposite end into a "V" shape. Beginning at folded end, glue Snowflakes and Letters to ribbon as shown, leaving about ¼" [6mm] between pieces. Hang as desired.

—Designed by Janna Britton

C – Letter "I"
(22w x 30h-hole piece)
Cut 1 & work.

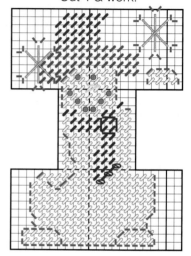

COLOR KEY: Winter Welcome

Metallic cord	Need-loft®	CORD AMOUNT
☐ Solid Silver	#21	3 yds. [2.7m]
☐ Gold Frizette	#34	2 yds. [1.8m]

Pearlized cord	Need-loft®	CORD AMOUNT
◩ White Iridescent	#33	5 yds. [4.6m]

Metallic thread	Kreinik	AMOUNT
■ Solid Pearl	#3200	6 yds. [5.5m]

Satin ribbon		AMOUNT
☐ White		¼ yd. [0.2m]

Pearl cotton or floss	DMC®	AMOUNT
■ Black	#310	1 yd. [0.9m]

Worsted-weight	Nylon Plus®	YARN AMOUNT
☐ Aqua Light	#39	30 yds. [27.4m]

Worsted-weight	Need-loft®	YARN AMOUNT
◩ White	#41	10 yds. [9.1m]
◪ Fern	#23	5 yds. [4.6m]
◪ Maple	#13	5 yds. [4.6m]
■ Red	#01	5 yds. [4.6m]
■ Royal	#32	4 yds. [3.7m]
■ Christmas Red	#02	3 yds. [2.7m]
■ Black	#00	2 yds. [1.8m]
■ Christmas Green	#28	2 yds. [1.8m]
■ Cinnamon	#14	1 yd. [0.9m]
■ Purple	#46	1 yd. [0.9m]
☐ Tangerine	#11	1 yd. [0.9m]
◩ Yellow	#57	1 yd. [0.9m]

STITCH KEY:
- ⊟ Backstitch/Straight
- ● French Knot
- ▧ Modified Turkey Work

D – Letter "N"
(22w x 30h-hole piece)
Cut 1 & work.

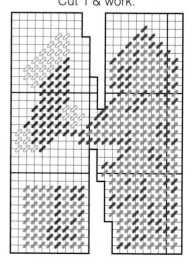

A – Snowflake
(6" Hexagon)
Cut 2 & leave unworked.

Cut out gray areas.

F – Letter "E"
(22w x 30h-hole piece)
Cut 1 & work.

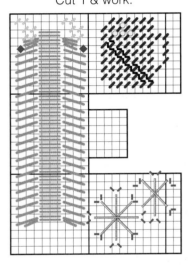

E – Letter "T"
(22w x 30h-hole piece)
Cut 1 & work.

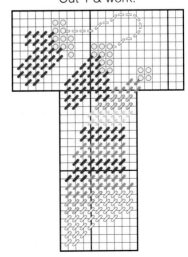

G – Letter "R"
(22w x 30h-hole piece)
Cut 1 & work.

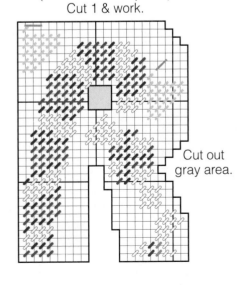

Cut out
gray area.

Snowman Tissue Cover

Melt away those winter
blues with this cool tissue cover.

SIZE: Snugly covers a boutique-style tissue box.

SKILL LEVEL: Average

MATERIALS:
• Three sheets of 7-mesh plastic canvas
• ¼ yd. [0.2m] length each of ⅛" [3mm] green and ¼" [6mm] red satin ribbon
• Craft glue or glue gun
• Heavy metallic braid or metallic cord; for amount see Color Key.

• Worsted-weight or plastic canvas yarn; for amounts see Color Keys.

CUTTING INSTRUCTIONS:
NOTE: Graphs continued on page 126.
A: For Cover Sides, cut four 29w x 37h-holes.
B: For Cover Top, cut one according to graph.
C: For Snowman, cut one according to graph.
D: For Broom, cut one according to graph.
E: For Wreath, cut one according to graph.

STITCHING INSTRUCTIONS:
1: Using colors and stitches indicated, work pieces according to graphs; fill in uncoded areas of C using white and continental stitch. With green, overcast cutout edges of B; with brown for Broom handle and with matching colors, overcast edges of C-E pieces.
2: Using yarn (Separate into individual plies, if desired.) and metallic braid or cord in colors and embroidery stitches indicated, embroider detail on C and E pieces as indicated on graphs.
NOTE: Cut one 4" [10.2cm] length of green.
3: Wrap green strand around Broom (see photo); glue ends at back to secure.
With green and herringbone whipstitch, whipstitch A and B pieces together; with herringbone overcast, overcast unfinished bottom edges.
4: Tie each ribbon length into a bow. Glue green bow to Snowman and red bow to Wreath as shown in photo. Matching bottom edges, glue Snowman to one Cover side; glue Wreath and Broom to Snowman as shown.

—Designed by Nancy Dorman

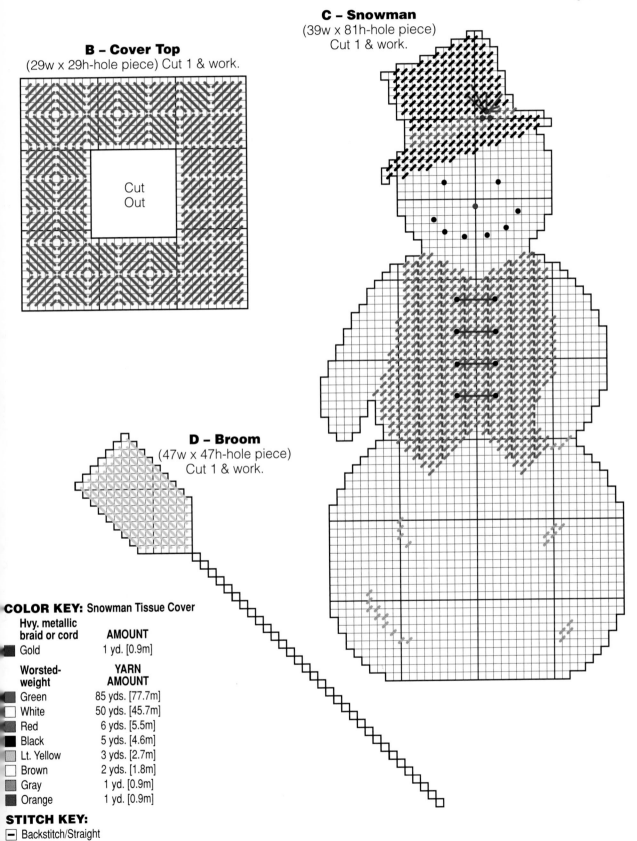

C – Snowman
(39w x 81h-hole piece)
Cut 1 & work.

B – Cover Top
(29w x 29h-hole piece) Cut 1 & work.

Cut
Out

D – Broom
(47w x 47h-hole piece)
Cut 1 & work.

COLOR KEY: Snowman Tissue Cover

Hvy. metallic braid or cord	AMOUNT
Gold	1 yd. [0.9m]

Worsted-weight	YARN AMOUNT
Green	85 yds. [77.7m]
White	50 yds. [45.7m]
Red	6 yds. [5.5m]
Black	5 yds. [4.6m]
Lt. Yellow	3 yds. [2.7m]
Brown	2 yds. [1.8m]
Gray	1 yd. [0.9m]
Orange	1 yd. [0.9m]

STITCH KEY:
- Backstitch/Straight
- French Knot

Snowman Treat Basket

This arctic friend has a tummy
full of sweet treats to share with all.

SIZE: 3½" x 7¼" x 7" tall [8.9cm x 18.4cm x 17.8cm].

SKILL LEVEL: Average

MATERIALS:
- 1½ sheets of 7-mesh plastic canvas
- Craft glue or glue gun
- Worsted-weight or plastic canvas yarn; for amounts see Color Keys.

CUTTING INSTRUCTIONS:
A: For Front, cut one according to graph.
B: For Back, cut one according to graph.
C: For Sides, cut two 20w x 22h-holes.
D: For Bottom, cut one 27w x 20h-holes (no graph).
E: For Arm #1 and #2, cut one each according to graphs.

STITCHING INSTRUCTIONS:
NOTE: D is not worked.
1: Using colors and stitches indicated, work A-C and E pieces according to graphs.
2: With white, whipstitch A-D pieces together according to Treat Basket Assembly Illustration; with matching colors as shown in photo, overcast unfinished edges.
3: With white, whipstitch E pieces right sides together as indicated; with matching colors as shown in photo, overcast unfinished edges.
4: Glue wrong side of Arms to Basket Back; bending Arms to Front as shown, glue hands to Basket Front.

—Designed by Dorothy Tabo

A – Front (37w x 20h-hole piece) Cut 1 & work.

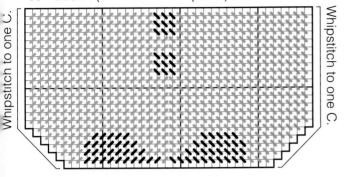

Whipstitch to one C.

Whipstitch to one C.

C – Side
(20w x 22h-hole pieces)
Cut 2 & work.

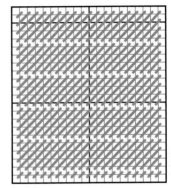

COLOR KEY: Snowman Treat Basket

Worsted-weight		YARN AMOUNT
	White	3 oz. [85.1g]
	Crimson	7 yds. [6.4m]
	Black	4 yds. [3.7m]
	Gold	4 yds. [3.7m]
	Orange	$1/4$ yd. [0.5m]

**Treat Basket
Assembly Illustration**
(Pieces are shown in
different colors for contrast;
gray denotes wrong side.)

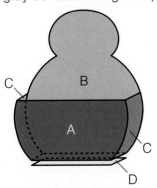

B – Back
(37w x 45h-hole piece) Cut 1 & work.

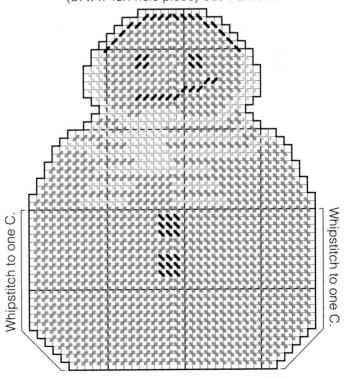

Whipstitch to one C.

Whipstitch to one C.

FROSTY FRIENDS

COLOR KEY: Snowman Treat Basket

Worsted-weight	YARN AMOUNT
White	3 oz. [85.1g]
Crimson	7 yds. [6.4m]
Black	4 yds. [3.7m]
Gold	4 yds. [3.7m]
Orange	1/4 yd. [0.5m]

E – Arm #1 (59w x 10h-hole piece) Cut 1 & work.

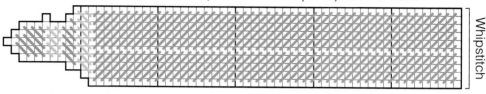

Whipstitch

E – Arm #2 (59w x 10h-hole piece) Cut 1 & work.

Whipstitch

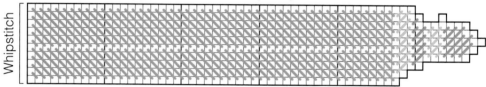

Snowman Tissue Cover

Instructions on page 122

COLOR KEY: Snowman Tissue Cover

Hvy. metallic braid or cord	AMOUNT
Gold	1 yd. [0.9m]

Worsted-weight	YARN AMOUNT
Green	85 yds. [77.7m]
White	50 yds. [45.7m]
Red	6 yds. [5.5m]
Black	5 yds. [4.6m]
Lt. Yellow	3 yds. [2.7m]
Brown	2 yds. [1.8m]
Gray	1 yd. [0.9m]
Orange	1 yd. [0.9m]

STITCH KEY:

- − Backstitch/Straight
- ● French Knot

E – Wreath
(19w x 19h-hole piece)
Cut 1 & work.

Cut Out

A – Cover Side
(29w x 37h-hole pieces) Cut 4 & work.

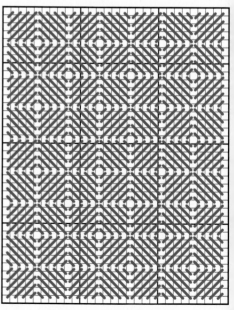

CHAPTER SIX

Elfin Magic

Prepare for the busy season by stitching a little magic. Who can resist these cheerful little elves as they light up your heart and home during this festive time of year? Each project is sure to become a family keepsake to be used year after year.

Elf Stocking

This Santa's helper will put
magic into your stocking this year.

SIZE: ¾" x 6" x 13" [1.9cm x 15.2cm x 33cm].

SKILL LEVEL: Average

MATERIALS:
- One Sheet of QuickCount® 7-mesh Plas[
  Canvas by Uniek, Inc.
- 1 yd. [0.9m] natural raffia
- One green ½" [13mm] tinsel pom-pom
- Craft glue or glue gun
- Needloft® Craft Cord by Uniek, Inc.; for
  amount see Color Key.
- Needloft® Yarn by Uniek, Inc. or worste[
  yarn; for amounts see Color Key.

CUTTING INSTRUCTIONS:
A: For Back, cut one according to graph.
B: For Front, cut one according to graph.
C: For Hands #1 and #2, cut one each
according to graphs.

STITCHING INSTRUCTIONS:
1: Using colors and stitches (Leave ¼"
[6mm] loops on modified turkey work
stitches.) indicated, work pieces according
to graphs. Omitting attachment edges, wit[
matching colors, overcast edges of pieces.
2: Using colors and stitches indicated,
embroider detail on A and B pieces as
indicated on graphs.
3: Holding wrong side of B to matching
edges on right side of A, with matching
colors, whipstitch together as indicated.
NOTE: Cut one ⅓-yd. [0.3m] length of
Christmas red yarn.
4: Wrap yarn strand around elf's neck an[
tie into a bow at front. Glue hands to Fro[
and pom-pom to hat on Back as shown i[
photo. Tie raffia into a bow and glue to
Front as shown. Display as desired.

—Designed by Kristine Loffre[

C – Hand #1 & #2
(8w x 6h-hole pieces)
Cut 1 each & work.

COLOR KEY: Elf Stocking

Metallic cord	Need-loft®	CORD AMOUNT
Iridescent Blue	#49	14 yds. [12.8m]

Worsted-weight	Need-loft®	YARN AMOUNT
Dark Royal	#48	12 yds. [11m]
Christmas Green	#28	7 yds. [6.4m]
Pink	#07	6 yds. [5.5m]
White	#41	3 yds. [2.7m]
Bittersweet	#52	2 yds. [1.8m]
Christmas Red	#02	2 yds. [1.8m]
Black	#00	1 yd. [0.9m]

STITCH KEY:
- Backstitch/Straight
- Modified Turkey Work

B – Front
(41w x 52h-hole piece) Cut 1 & work.

A – Back
(41w x 87h-hole piece)
Cut 1 & work.

Leave unworked.

Whipstitch to B between arrows.

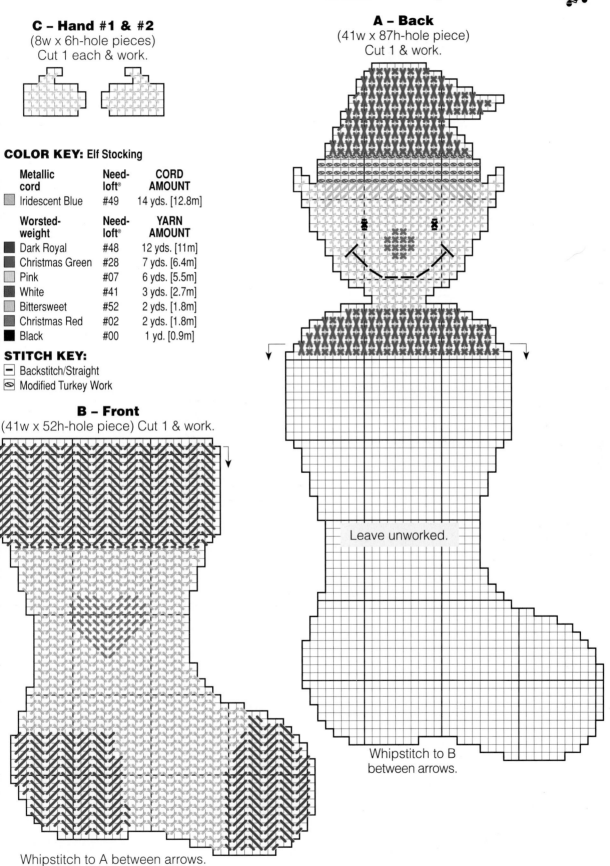

Whipstitch to A between arrows.

Christmas Ornaments

*These delightful ornaments are
sure to set the mood for a childlike Christmas.*

SIZES: Elf is ¾" x 4" x 8" [1.9cm x 10.2cm x 20.3cm]; Lion is ¾" x 3½" x 8½" [1.9cm x 8.9cm x 21.6cm]; Snowman is ¾" x 5" x 5¼" [1.9cm x 12.7cm x 13.3cm]; Santa is ¾" x 3½" x 8⅛" [1.9cm x 8.9cm x 20.6cm].

SKILL LEVEL: Challenging

MATERIALS FOR ONE:
- One sheet of 7-mesh plastic canvas
- **For Elf:** ¼-sheet of black felt; One ⅜" [10mm] and five ¼" [6mm] gold jingle bells; 1 yd. [0.9m] natural ½" [13mm] decorative lace; One red ⅜" [10mm] heart shank button (cut away shank and file nub smooth); Two black seed beads; One red ¼" [6mm] wooden bead
- **For Lion:** Two brown/black ⅛" [3mm] animal eyes; One small artificial animal nose; ⅓ yd. [0.3m] red ⅛" [3mm] satin ribbon; One small Christmas charm of choice; Three white ¼" [6mm] sew-on buttons
- **For Snowman:** Two black seed beads; Scraps of yellow and blue felt; Three black ¼" [6mm] faceted beads; Two 2"-long [5.1cm] twigs; One baby's sock cuff
- **For Santa:** Two black seed beads; One red ¼" [6mm] wooden bead; One gold ⅜" x ⅝" [10mm x 16mm] buckle from a wristwatch; Small Amounts of White, Black and Plush White Felt by Kunin Felt; One white ⅜" [10mm] and three white ¼" [6mm] sew-on buttons
- Sewing needle
- Pinking shears (for Elf and Santa)
- Craft glue or glue gun
- Six-strand embroidery floss; for amount see individual Color Keys.
- Worsted-weight or plastic canvas yarn; for amounts see individual Color Keys.

ELF
CUTTING INSTRUCTIONS:
A: For Head Front and Back, cut one eac[h] according to graphs.
B: For Body Front and Back, cut two (on[e] for Front and one for Back) according to graph.
C: For Arm Pieces, cut four 2w x 18h-hol[e]
D: For Leg Pieces, cut four according to graph.

STITCHING INSTRUCTIONS:
1: Using colors indicated and continental stitch, work pieces according to graphs. Omitting attachment edges, with fern, overcast edges of B pieces.
2: Using two strands floss and yarn (Separate into individual plies, if desired.) in colors and embroidery stitches (Leave [6mm] loops on modified turkey work stitches.) indicated, embroider detail on A pieces as indicated on graphs. With two strands floss, sew seed and wooden bead to Front A as indicated.
3: With matching colors, whipstitch A pieces wrong sides together; with fern, whipstitch B pieces wrong sides together as indicated. For each Arm (make 2), with matching colors, whipstitch two C pieces wrong sides together; for each Leg (make 2), whipstitch two D pieces wrong sides together.
NOTE: For Boot Cuffs, with pinking shea[rs] cut two 1½"-across [3.8cm] circles from black felt; cut a ⅜" [10mm] slit in center of each circle.
4: Place one Boot Cuff on each Leg; inser[t] Legs inside bottom of Body (see photo) and glue to secure. Insert neck of Head inside top of Body and glue to secure.
5: Glue decorative lace around hat brim,

sleeves and neck as shown in photo, trimming excess as needed to fit. Glue Arms to Body as shown. Glue large jingle bell to hat and small bells to Body and Legs as shown; glue heart button to Body as shown. Hang as desired.

LION

CUTTING INSTRUCTIONS:

A: For Head Front and Back, cut one each according to graphs.

B: For Body Front and Back, cut two (one for Front and one for Back) according to graph.

C: For Arm Pieces, cut four 2w x 18h-holes (no graph).

D: For Leg Pieces, cut four according to graph.

E: For Muzzle, cut one according to graph.

F: For Pocket, cut one according to graph.

G: For Ears, cut two 3w x 2h-holes.

STITCHING INSTRUCTIONS:

1: Using colors indicated and continental stitch, work A, B and D-F pieces according to graphs; using yellow and continental stitch, work C pieces. Omitting attachment edges, with yellow for Ears and with matching colors, overcast edges of B and E-G pieces.

2: Using two strands floss and yarn (Separate into individual plies, if desired.) in colors and embroidery stitches (Leave ¼" [6mm] loops on modified turkey work

stitches.) indicated, embroider detail on Front A and E pieces as indicated on graphs. With two strands floss, sew button to one B for Front (see photo).

NOTE: Cut twenty-five 4" [10.2cm] length of yellow.

3: With yellow, whipstitch A pieces wrong sides together. For mane, attach one 4" length with a Lark's Head Knot to each ▲ hole around Head; pull ends to even and trim and fray ends to fluff. Cut through loops on Head Front; trim and fray ends to fluff.

NOTE: Cut four 9" [22.9cm] lengths of yellow.

4: For Tail, hold cut strands together and thread from front to back through one ◆ hole on Back B, then from back to front through adjacent ◆ hole on Back B. Pull ends to even and twist strands together; tie ends into a knot to secure. With yellow

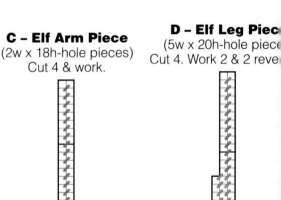

B – Elf Body Front & Back
(15w x 19h-hole pieces)
Cut 2. Work for Front & 1 for Back.

Whipstitch between arrows.

A – Elf Head B
(14w x 19h-hole p
Cut 1 & work

COLOR KEY: Elf

Embroidery floss	**AMOUNT**
■ Black	¼ yd. [0.2m]

Worsted-weight	**YARN AMOUNT**
Fern	15 yds. [13.7m]
Black	2 yds. [1.8m]
Rust	6 yds. [5.5m]
Pink	1 yd. [0.9m]
Dk. Pink	¼ yd. [0.2m]

OTHER:
- ⊟ Backstitch/Straight
- ⊠ Modified Turkey Work
- Ⓞ Seed Bead Attachment
- Ⓞ Red Wooden Bead Attachment

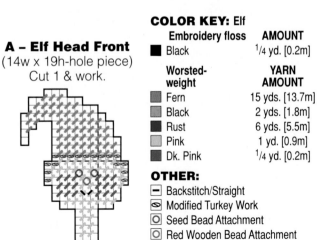

A – Elf Head Front
(14w x 19h-hole piece)
Cut 1 & work.

C – Elf Arm Piece
(2w x 18h-hole pieces)
Cut 4 & work.

D – Elf Leg Piec
(5w x 20h-hole piece
Cut 4. Work 2 & 2 rever

hipstitch B pieces wrong sides together
indicated.

For each Arm (make 2), whipstitch two
pieces wrong sides together; for each
g (make 2), whipstitch two D pieces
ong sides together. Insert Legs inside
ottom of Body (see photo) and glue to
cure. Insert neck of Head inside top of
dy and glue to secure.

Glue animal eyes, Ears and Muzzle to
ead and nose to Muzzle as shown. Glue
arm to wrong side of Pocket and Pocket
d Arms to Body as shown.

Tie ribbon into a bow around knot
 tail, trimming excess as needed. Tie
mainder of ribbon into a bow around
on's neck as shown; trim excess as
eded. Hang as desired.

NOWMAN
UTTING INSTRUCTIONS:
For Head Front and Back, cut one each
cording to graphs.
For Body Front and Back, cut two
ne for Front and one for Back) according
 graph.
For Mitten Pieces, cut four from blue
lt according to Mitten Cutting Guide
 page 135.

ITCHING INSTRUCTIONS:
Using colors indicated and continental
tch, work A and B pieces according to
aphs. Omitting attachment edges, with
hite, overcast edges of B pieces.
Using two strands floss and backstitch,
mbroider mouth on Front A as indicated
 graph. With two strands floss, sew seed
ads to Front A as indicated; sew faceted
ads to one B for Front as shown in photo.
With white, whipstitch A pieces wrong
es together; whipstitch B pieces wrong
es together as indicated.
Insert neck of Head inside top of Body
d glue to secure. For each Mitten (make
, glue two C pieces together at matching
ges over one end of one twig. Glue
posite end of one twig inside each small

opening at sides of Body (see photo).
NOTE: Cut one ¾" x 6" [1.9cm x 15.2cm]
length from yellow felt; snip each short end
to form a scarf.

5: Wrap scarf around Snowman's neck as
shown and glue to secure. Fashion a hat
from baby's cuff sock and glue to Snowman's head as shown. Hang as desired.

SANTA
CUTTING INSTRUCTIONS:
A: For Head Front and Back, cut one each
according to graphs.
B: For Body Front and Back, cut two
(one for Front and one for Back) according
to graph.
C: For Arm Pieces, cut four 2w x 18h-holes.
D: For Leg Pieces, cut four according
to graph.
E: For Mustache, Beard, Hair Front and
Hair Back, cut one each from white felt
according to corresponding Cutting Guides.

STITCHING INSTRUCTIONS:
1: Using colors indicated and continental
stitch, work A-D pieces according to
graphs. Omitting attachment edges, with
red, overcast edges of B pieces.
2: Using red yarn and French knot, embroider mouth on Front A as indicated on
graph. With two strands floss, sew seed
and wooden beads to Front A as indicated;
sew buttons to one B for Front (see photo).
3: With white for hair area and with matching colors, whipstitch A pieces wrong sides
together; with red, whipstitch B pieces
wrong sides together as indicated. For
each Arm (make 2), with matching colors,
whipstitch two C pieces wrong sides
together; for each Leg (make 2), whipstitch
two D pieces wrong sides together.
4: Insert Legs inside bottom of Body (see
photo) and glue to secure. Insert neck of
Head inside top of Body and glue to secure.
Glue Mustache, Beard, Hair Front and Hair
Back around Head as shown in photo.
NOTE: Cut one ⅜" x 14" [1cm x 35.6cm]
length of plush white felt; cut one ⅜" x ⅝"

[10mm x 16mm] piece of black felt.
5: Glue plush white felt strip around
hat brim on Head, around each sleeve
area on Arms, around hip area on
Body and around each boot cuff area
on Legs as shown in photo, trimming
excess as needed to fit. Thread black
felt piece through belt buckle and glue
to Body as shown. Glue large white
button to hat tip on Head as shown.
Hang as desired.

—*Designed by Lee Lindeman*

A – Santa Head Front
(14w x 19h-hole piece)
Cut 1 & work.

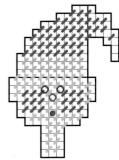

A – Santa Head Back
(14w x 19h-hole piece)
Cut 1 & work.

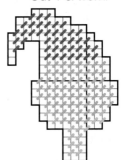

B – Santa Body Front & Back
(15w x 19h-hole pieces)
Cut 2. Work 1 for Front & 1 for Back.

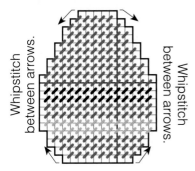

D – Santa Leg Piece
(5w x 20h-hole pieces)
Cut 4. Work 2 & 2 reversed.

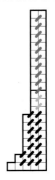

COLOR KEY: Santa

Worsted-weight	YARN AMOUNT
Red	15 yds. [13.7m]
White	2 yds. [1.8m]
Black	1 yd. [0.9m]
Pink	1 yd. [0.9m]
Dk. Pink	1/4 yd. [0.2m]

OTHER:
◉ French Knot
◙ Seed Bead Attachment
◙ Wood Bead Attachment

C – Santa Arm Piece
(2w x 18h-hole pieces)
Cut 4 & work.

**Santa
Hair Front Cutting Guide**
(actual size)

Cut with pinking shears
between arrows.

Santa Hair Back Cutting Guide
(actual size)

**Santa
Beard Cutting Gu...**
(actual size)

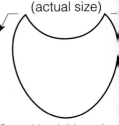

Cut with pinking she...
between arrows.

**Santa
Mustache Cutting Guide**
(actual size)

COLOR KEY: Lion

Embroidery floss	AMOUNT
■ Black	¼ yd. [0.2m]

Worsted-weight	YARN AMOUNT
☐ Yellow	25 yds. [22.9m]
◪ Eggshell	1 yd. [0.9m]
■ Dk. Pink	¼ yd. [0.2m]

OTHER:
- ⊟ Backstitch/Straight
- ⊠ Modified Turkey Work
- Lark's Head Knot
- ◆ Tail Attachment

F – Lion Pocket
(4w x 4h-hole piece)
Cut 1 & work.

E – Lion Muzzle
(5w x 4h-hole piece)
Cut 1 & work.

G – Lion Ear
(3w x 2h-hole pieces)
Cut 2 & work.

A – Lion Head Back
(11w x 14h-hole piece)
Cut 1 & work.

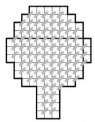

B – Lion Body Front & Back
(15w x 19h-hole pieces)
Cut 2. Work 1 for Front & 1 for Back.

Whipstitch between arrows.

Whipstitch between arrows.

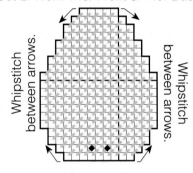

D – Lion Leg Piece
(5 w x 19h-hole pieces)
Cut 4. Work 2 & 2 reversed.

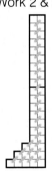

A – Lion Head Front
(11w x 14h-hole piece)
Cut 1 & work.

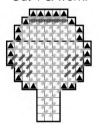

COLOR KEY: Snowman

Embroidery floss	AMOUNT
■ Black	¼ yd. [0.2m]

Worsted-weight	YARN AMOUNT
▨ White	12 yds. [11m]
■ Dk. Pink	½ yd. [0.5m]

OTHER:
- ⊟ Backstitch/Straight
- ⊙ Seed Bead Attachment

Snowman Mitten Cutting Guide
(actual size)

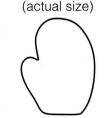

B – Snowman Body Front & Back
(15w x 19h-hole pieces)
Cut 2. Work 1 for Front & 1 for Back.

Whipstitch   Whipstitch

Whipstitch between arrows.

Whipstitch between arrows.

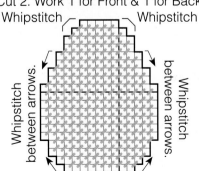

A – Snowman Head Front
(11w x 14h-hole piece)
Cut 1 & work.

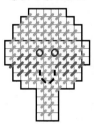

A – Snowman Head Back
(11w x 14h-hole piece)
Cut 1 & work.

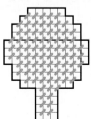

Star Coasters and Bowl

*Create a celestial centerpiece
with this brilliant coaster and bowl set.*

ZES: Each Coaster is 5" x 5" [12.7cm x 2.7cm]; Holder is 1½" x 3½" x 2¼" tall .8cm x 8.9cm x 5.7cm]; Bowl is 8½" x ½" x 5" tall [21.6cm x 21.6cm x 12.7cm].

KILL LEVEL: Average

ATERIALS:
Fifteen 5" [12.7cm] QuickShape™ Plastic Canvas Star Shapes by Uniek, Inc.
¼ Sheet of QuickCount® 7-mesh Plastic Canvas by Uniek, Inc.
Two 9" x 12" [22.9cm x 30.5cm] sheets of white felt
Fabri-Tac™ Fabric Glue by Beacon™ Chemical Co. or craft glue
Needloft® Craft Cord by Uniek, Inc.; for amount see Color Key.
Needloft® Yarn by Uniek, Inc. or worsted yarn; for amounts see Color Key.

UTTING INSTRUCTIONS:
: For Coaster Fronts and Backings, cut ight (four for Fronts and four for Backings) om star shapes according to graph.
: For Coaster Holder Sides, cut apart one ar shape according to graph.
: For Coaster Holder Ends, cut two from -mesh 9w x 11h-holes.
: For Coaster Holder Bottom Pieces, ut two from 7-mesh 11w x 9h-holes.

E: For Bowl Sides, use five star shapes.
F: For Bowl Bottom, use remaining star shape.

STITCHING INSTRUCTIONS:
NOTE: Four A pieces are not worked for Backings.
1: Using colors and stitches indicated, work pieces according to graphs. For each Coaster (make 4), holding one Backing to wrong side each Front, with white worsted-weight, whipstitch together. For Coaster Holder, whipstitch B-D pieces wrong sides together according to Holder Assembly Illustration; overcast unfinished edges.
NOTE: Using E pieces as a pattern, cut six linings from felt ⅛" [3mm] smaller at all edges; cut ten ¼" x 3" [0.6cm x 7.6cm] strips of felt.
2: For Bowl, whipstitch E and F pieces wrong sides together as indicated on graphs; overcast unfinished edges. For lining, glue one felt star to wrong side of Bowl Bottom and each Bowl Side; glue one strip over each joining edge to conceal.

—*Designed by Carole Rodgers*

C – Coaster Holder End
(9w x 11h-hole pieces)
Cut 2 from 7-mesh & work.

A – Coaster Front & Backing
(5" stars)
Cut 8. Work 4 for Fronts & leave 4 unworked for Backings.

Cut away gray area.

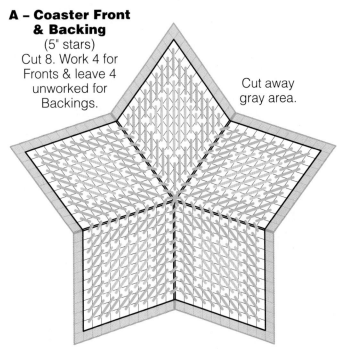

COLOR KEY: Star Coasters & Bowl

Pearlized cord	Need-loft®	CORD AMOUNT
☐ White	#43	40 yds. [36.6m]

Worsted-weight	Need-loft®	YARN AMOUNT
☐ White	#41	75 yds. [68.6m]

ELFIN MAGIC

F – Bowl Bottom
Use remaining 5"
star shape & work.

Whipstitch
to one A.

Whipstitch
to one A.

Whipstitch
to one A.

Whipstitch
to one A.

Whipstitch
to one A.

**D – Coaster Holder
Bottom Piece**
(11w x 9h-hole pieces)
Cut 2 from 7-mesh & work.

**Holder
Assembly
Illustration**
(Gray denotes
wrong side.)

C
B
B
C
D

**B – Coaster
Holder Side**
(5" star)
Cut apart 1.
Work 2 sections.

Cut away
gray area.

Cut
Line

E – Bowl Side
Use five 5" star
shapes & work.

Whipstitch

Whipstitch

Whipstitch to B.

COLOR KEY: Star Coasters & Bowl

	Pearlized cord	Need-loft®	CORD AMOUNT
☐	White	#43	40 yds. [36.6m]
	Worsted-weight	Need-loft®	YARN AMOUNT
☐	White	#41	75 yds. [68.6m]

Elf Napkin Ring

Add fun and festivity to
your table with this playful pixie.

ZE: 2" across x 4" [5.1cm x 10.2cm].

KILL LEVEL: Average

ATERIALS:
½ Sheet of QuickCount® 7-mesh Plastic
Canvas by Uniek, Inc.
One red ¼" [6mm] pom-pom
Craft glue or glue gun
Needloft® Yarn by Uniek, Inc. or worsted
yarn; for amounts see Color Key.

UTTING INSTRUCTIONS:
: For Elf Motif, cut one according to graph.
: For Bow Tie, cut one according to graph.
: For Napkin Band, cut one 44w x
n-holes.

TITCHING INSTRUCTIONS:
: Using colors and stitches (Leave ¼"
mm] loops on modified turkey work
itches.) indicated, work pieces according
graphs. With matching colors, overcast
dges of pieces.
: Using colors and embroidery stitches
dicated, embroider detail on A as
dicated on graph.

3: Glue Bow Tie and pom-pom to Elf
Motif as shown; glue Elf Motif over seam
on Napkin Band. Cut through loops on
Elf Motif; trim and fray ends to fluff,
forming hat band.

—Designed by Kristine Loffredo

OLOR KEY: Elf Napkin Ring

Worsted-weight	Need-loft®	YARN AMOUNT
White	#41	5 yds. [4.6m]
Christmas Green	#28	2 yds. [1.8m]
Red	#01	2 yds. [1.8m]
Bittersweet	#52	1 yd. [0.9m]
Orchid	#44	1 yd. [0.9m]
Brown	#15	¼ yd. [0.2m]

TITCH KEY:
: Backstitch/Straight
: French Knot
: Modified Turkey Work

B – Bow Tie
(4w x 4h-hole piece)
Cut 1 & work.

C – Napkin Band
(44w x 4h-hole piece)
Cut 1 & work, overlapping ends &
working through both thicknesses
at overlap area to join.

Lap
Over

Lap
Under

A – Elf Motif
(11w x 25h-hole piece)
Cut 1 & work.

Elf Frame

Capture a magical moment
and display it in this merry Elf Frame.

SIZE: 4½" x 6½" [11.4cm x 16.5cm], not including embellishments, with a 3¼" x 5⅛" [8.3cm x 13cm] photo window.

SKILL LEVEL: Average

MATERIALS:
- One Sheet of QuickCount® 7-mesh Plastic Canvas by Uniek, Inc.
- Two gold ¼" [6mm] jingle bells
- One red ¼" [6mm] pom-pom
- Four 15mm x 20mm green holly leaf sequins
- Two red 8mm round faceted beads
- Craft glue or glue gun

- Needloft® Craft Cord by Uniek, Inc.; for amount see Color Key.
- Needloft® Yarn by Uniek, Inc. or worsted yarn; for amounts see Color Key.

CUTTING INSTRUCTIONS:
A: For Frame Front, cut one according to graph.
B: For Frame Back, cut one 41w x 27h-holes (no graph).
C: For Frame Stand, cut one according to graph.
D: For Elf, cut one according to graph.
E: For Arms, cut one according to graph.

STITCHING INSTRUCTIONS:

NOTE: B and C pieces are not worked.

1: Using colors and stitches indicated, work A (omit stitches within attachment edges), D (Leave ¼" [6mm] loops on modified turkey work stitches.) and E pieces according to graphs. With cord, overcast cutout edges of A; with forest, overcast outer edges of A. Omitting attachment edges, with matching colors, overcast edges of D and E pieces.

2: Using colors and embroidery stitches indicated, embroider detail on D and E pieces as indicated on graphs.

3: Whipstitch A-C pieces together as indicated and according to Frame Assembly Diagram. With red, whipstitch E to right side of D as indicated; glue Arms to Elf to secure (see photo).

NOTE: Cut one 9" [22.9cm] length of yellow yarn; tie into a bow and trim ends.

4: Glue pom-pom to tip of hat and one bell to tip of each shoe on Elf as shown; glue Elf to one corner of Frame and bow to Elf as shown. Glue two holly leaves and one bead to each of two corners on Frame as shown.

—Designed by Kristine Loffredo

C – Frame Stand
(8w x 24h-hole piece)
Cut 1 & leave unworked.

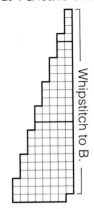

Whipstitch to B.

Frame Assembly Diagram
(Pieces are shown in different colors for contrast; gray denotes wrong side.)

Step 1:
With forest, whipstitch C to center of B at matching bottom edges.

Step 2:
Holding B to wrong side of A, work remaining stitches within attachment edges according to A graph.

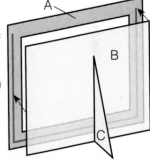

COLOR KEY: Elf Frame

Metallic cord	Need-loft®	CORD AMOUNT
Gold	#01	5 yds. [4.6m]

Worsted-weight	Need-loft®	YARN AMOUNT
Forest	#29	7 yds. [6.4m]
Christmas Green	#28	3 yds. [2.7m]
Red	#01	2 yds. [1.8m]
Bittersweet	#52	1 yd. [0.9m]
Orchid	#44	1 yd. [0.9m]
Royal	#32	1 yd. [0.9m]
Cinnamon	#14	¼ yd. [0.2m]
White	#41	¼ yd. [0.2m]
Yellow	#57	¼ yd. [0.2m]

OTHER:
- Backstitch/Straight
- Modified Turkey Work
- Frame Back Attachment

E – Arms
(13w x 13h-hole piece)
Cut 1 & work.

Whipstitch to D.

D – Elf
(23w x 19h-hole piece)
Cut 1 & work.

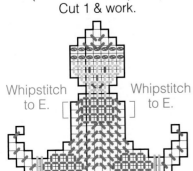

Whipstitch to E.   Whipstitch to E.

A – Frame Front
(43w x 30h-hole piece) Cut 1 & work.

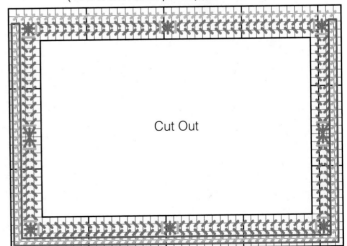

Cut Out

Elf Door Hanger

Fun times are sure to abound
with this happy character hanging around.

ZE: 8" x 12¾" [20.3cm x 32.4cm].

KILL LEVEL: Easy

ATERIALS:

One Sheet of QuickCount® 7-mesh
Plastic Canvas by Uniek, Inc.
Two red ½" [13mm] sew-on buttons
Sewing needle
No. 5 Pearl Cotton Art. 116 by DMC® or
six-strand embroidery floss; for amounts
see Color Key.
Needloft® Yarn by Uniek, Inc. or worsted
yarn; for amounts see Color Key.

UTTING INSTRUCTIONS:

or Elf, cut one according to graph.

TITCHING INSTRUCTIONS:

: Using colors indicated and continental
itch, work Elf according to graph. With
atching colors, overcast edges.
: Using pearl cotton or three strands floss
 colors and embroidery stitches indicated,

embroider detail on Elf as indicated
on graph.
3: With bt. red pearl cotton or floss, sew
buttons to Elf as indicated.

—Designed by Michele Wilcox

Elf
(52w x 83h-hole piece)
Cut 1 & work.

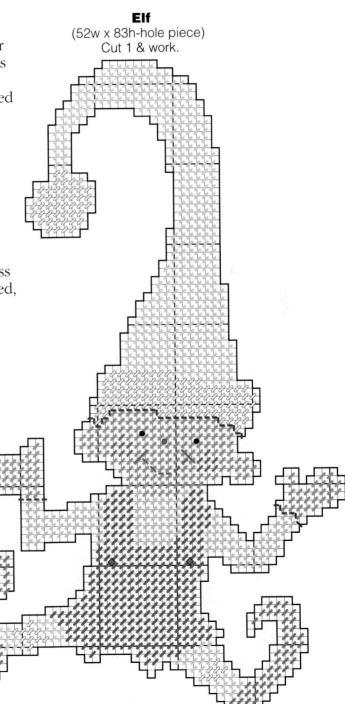

COLOR KEY: Elf Door Hanger

Pearl cotton or floss	DMC®	AMOUNT
Vy. Lt. Beige Brown	#842	2 yds. [1.8m]
Black	#310	¼ yd. [0.2m]
Bt. Red	#666	¼ yd. [0.2m]

Worsted-weight	Need-loft®	YARN AMOUNT
Red	#01	10 yds. [9.1m]
Flesh Tone	#56	7 yds. [6.4m]
Royal	#32	7 yds. [6.4m]
Christmas Green	#28	5 yds. [4.6m]
White	#41	5 yds. [4.6m]
Yellow	#57	5 yds. [4.6m]
Pink	#07	1 yd. [0.9m]

OTHER:

- Backstitch/Straight
● French Knot
◆ Button Attachment

Star Frame

*Show off the stars of your
life in these brightly colored frames.*

SIZE: Each is 5" x 5⅜" [12.7cm x 13.7cm],
including hanger, and with a 3"-across
[7.6cm] photo opening.

SKILL LEVEL: Average

MATERIALS FOR ONE:
• Two 5" [12.7cm] QuickShape™ Plastic
Canvas Star Shapes by Uniek, Inc.

• Five desired-color 15mm foil-backed
acrylic star stones
• Craft glue or glue gun
• Metallic cord; for amount see Color Key
• Worsted-weight or plastic canvas yarn;
for amount see Color Key.

CUTTING INSTRUCTIONS:
A: For Frame Front, cut one from one

star shape according to graph (do not remove hanger).

B: For Frame Back, cut one from remaining star shape according to graph.

STITCHING INSTRUCTIONS:

NOTE: B is not worked.

1: Using colors and stitches indicated, work A according to graph. With cord, overcast cutout edges.

NOTE: Using A as a pattern, trim photo ⅛" [3mm] smaller at all edges.

2: Holding B to wrong side of A, omitting hanger on A and with cord, whipstitch outer edges together, inserting photo before closing. Glue star stones to Front as shown in photo.

—Designed by Kimberly Suber

COLOR KEY: Star Frame	
Metallic cord	**AMOUNT**
▨ Desired-color	8 yds. [7.3m]
Worsted-weight	**YARN AMOUNT**
▨ Desired-color	5 yds. [4.6m]

B – Frame Back
(5" star)
Cut 1 from remaining star shape & leave unworked.

Cut out gray areas.

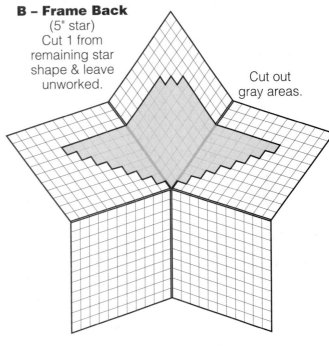

A – Frame Front
(5" star)
Cut 1 from one star shape & work.

Cut out gray area.

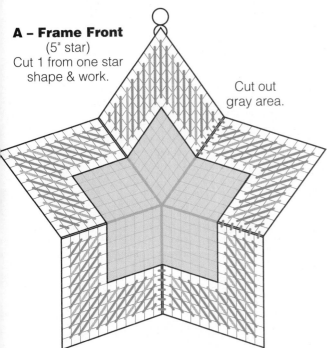

Christmas Money Tree

Make giving more fun
with this clever Christmas cash idea.

SIZE: 13½" x 12¾" tall [34.3cm x 32.4cm].

SKILL LEVEL: Average

MATERIALS FOR ONE:
- One Sheet of Green QuickCount® 7-mesh Plastic Canvas by Uniek, Inc.
- Craft glue or glue gun

- Needloft® Craft Cord by Uniek, Inc.; for amount see Color Key.

CUTTING INSTRUCTIONS:
A: For Tree, cut one according to graph.
B: For Star Front, cut one according to graph.
C: For Star Backing, cut one according to graph.

B – Star Front
(16w x 16h-hole piece)
Cut 1 & work.

Cut Out

Whipstitch to C
between arrows.

STITCHING INSTRUCTIONS:

NOTE: A and C pieces are not worked.

Using cord and continental stitch, work according to graph; overcast cutout edges.

Holding C to wrong side of B, with cord, whipstitch together as indicated, forming Star; overcast unfinished edges of B.

Glue Star to Tree top (see photo). Star holds a dollar coin; Tree holds paper bills of any denomination. Hang as desired.

—*Designed by Sandra Miller Maxfield*

A – Tree
(89w x 70h-hole piece)
Cut 1 & leave unworked.

Cut out gray areas.

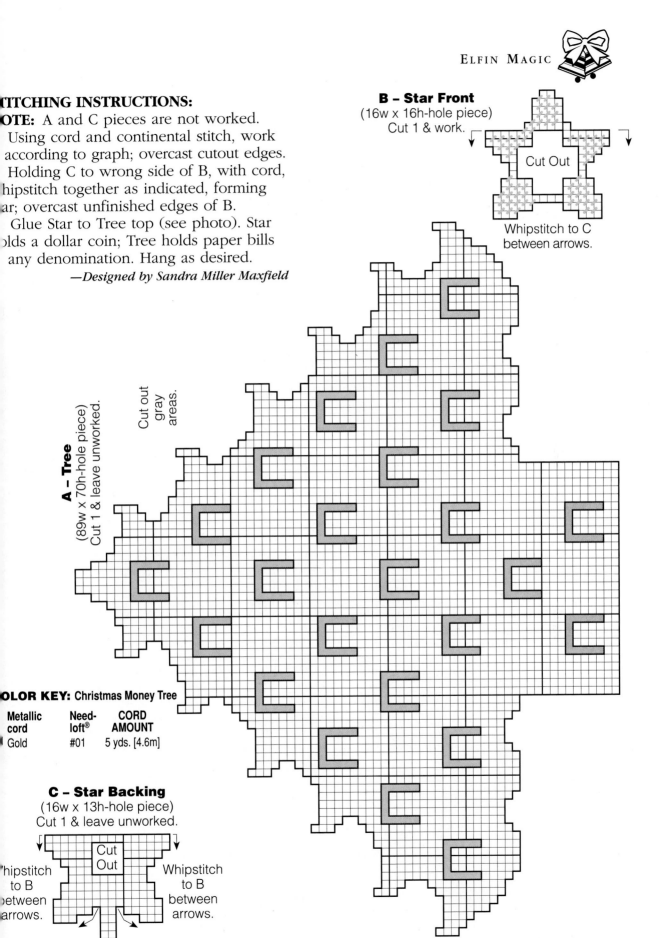

COLOR KEY: Christmas Money Tree

Metallic cord	Need-loft®	CORD AMOUNT
Gold	#01	5 yds. [4.6m]

C – Star Backing
(16w x 13h-hole piece)
Cut 1 & leave unworked.

Cut Out

Whipstitch to B between arrows.

Whipstitch to B between arrows.

Elf Doorstop

Let this jolly little elf invite
guests into any room in your house.

SIZE: 3" x 12" x 9¾" tall [7.6cm x 30.5cm x 24.8cm].

SKILL LEVEL: Average

MATERIALS:
- Two Sheets of QuickCount® 7-mesh Plastic Canvas by Uniek, Inc.
- ⅓ yd. [0.3m] natural raffia

Two silver ⅜" [10mm] jingle bells
One red 1" [2.5cm] pom-pom
Zip-close bag filled with gravel or other weighting material
Craft glue or glue gun
Needloft® Craft Cord by Uniek, Inc.; for amount see Color Key.
Needloft® Yarn by Uniek, Inc. or worsted yarn; for amounts see Color Key.

UTTING INSTRUCTIONS:

: For Back, cut one according to graph.

: For Front, cut one 56w x 27h-holes.

: For Sides, cut two 16w x 27h-holes.

): For Top and Bottom, cut two (one for op and one for Bottom) 56w x 16h-holes.

: For Nose, cut one according to graph.

: For Hands #1 and #2, cut one each ccording to graphs.

: For Bow Tie, cut one according) graph.

: For Heart, cut one according to graph.

TITCHING INSTRUCTIONS:

: Using colors and stitches (Leave ¼" mm] loops on modified turkey work titches.) indicated, work pieces according) graphs. Omitting attachment edges, with d for Bow Tie and with matching colors, vercast edges of A and E-H pieces.

: Using black and stitches indicated,

embroider detail on A as indicated on graph. With sail blue, whipstitch B-D pieces together, forming Cover assembly; whipstitch assembly to right side of A as indicated, inserting weighting material before closing.

NOTE: Cut raffia into six 6" [15.2cm] lengths.

3: Holding raffia lengths together, tie a knot in center; trim and fray ends as desired (see photo). Glue raffia knot to Front and Heart over raffia knot as shown in photo. Glue pom-pom to hat tip and Nose and Bow Tie to Back; glue one bell to tip of each shoe on Back as shown.

—Designed by Kristine Loffredo

COLOR KEY: Elf Doorstop

Metallic cord	Need-loft®	CORD AMOUNT
Gold	#01	8 yds. [7.3m]

Worsted-weight	Need-loft®	YARN AMOUNT
Sail Blue	#35	39 yds. [35.7m]
Christmas Green	#28	16 yds. [14.6m]
Orchid	#44	8 yds. [7.3m]
Red	#01	7 yds. [6.4m]
Maple	#13	2 yds. [1.8m]
Black	#00	1 yd. [0.9m]
White	#41	1 yd. [0.9m]

OTHER:
- Backstitch/Straight
- Modified Turkey Work
- Cover Attachment

B – Front
(56w x 27h-hole piece) Cut 1 & work.

C – Side
(16w x 27h-hole pieces)
Cut 2 & work.

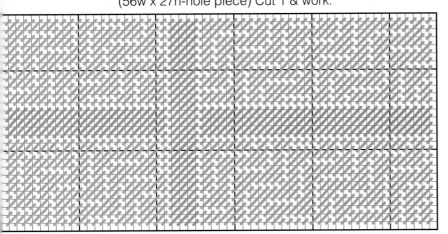

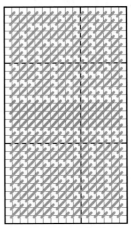

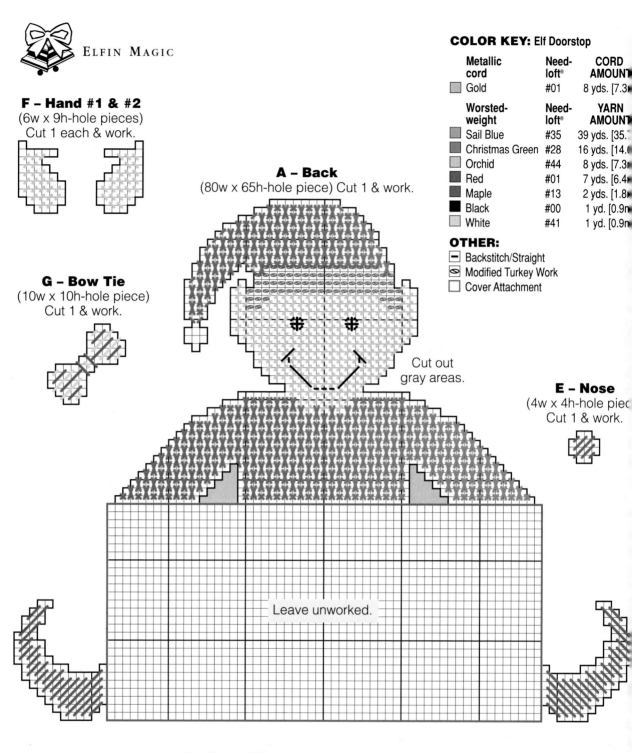

ELFIN MAGIC

F – Hand #1 & #2
(6w x 9h-hole pieces)
Cut 1 each & work.

G – Bow Tie
(10w x 10h-hole piece)
Cut 1 & work.

A – Back
(80w x 65h-hole piece) Cut 1 & work.

Cut out
gray areas.

E – Nose
(4w x 4h-hole piec)
Cut 1 & work.

Leave unworked.

COLOR KEY: Elf Doorstop

Metallic cord	Need-loft®	CORD AMOUNT
Gold	#01	8 yds. [7.3

Worsted-weight	Need-loft®	YARN AMOUNT
Sail Blue	#35	39 yds. [35.
Christmas Green	#28	16 yds. [14.
Orchid	#44	8 yds. [7.3
Red	#01	7 yds. [6.4
Maple	#13	2 yds. [1.8
Black	#00	1 yd. [0.9
White	#41	1 yd. [0.9

OTHER:
- Backstitch/Straight
- Modified Turkey Work
- Cover Attachment

D – Top & Bottom
(56w x 16h-hole pieces)
Cut 2. Work 1 for Top & leave 1 unworked for Bottom.

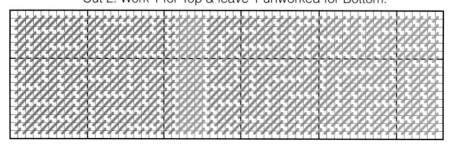

H – Heart
(15w x 14h-hole piece)
Cut 1 & work.

Elf Treat Holder

*Let Santa's helper hand
out treats at your holiday parties.*

SIZE: 2" x 6½" x 6" tall [5.1cm x 16.5cm 15.2cm].

SKILL LEVEL: Average

MATERIALS:
One Sheet of QuickCount® 7-mesh
Plastic Canvas by Uniek, Inc.
One red ½" [13mm] tinsel pom-pom
Craft glue or glue gun
Needloft® Yarn by Uniek, Inc. or worsted
yarn; for amounts see Color Key.

CUTTING INSTRUCTIONS:
For Back, cut one according to graph.
For Front and Bottom, cut two (one
for Front and one for Bottom) according
to graph.
For Sides, cut two according to graph.
For Nose, cut one according to graph.
For Collar, cut one according to graph.
For Arms #1 and #2, cut one each
according to graphs.
For Foot #1 and #2, cut one each
according to graph.
For Holly, cut one according to graph.

STITCHING INSTRUCTIONS:
Using colors and stitches (Leave ¼"
[6mm] loops on modified turkey work
stitches.) indicated, work pieces according
to graphs. Omitting attachment edges, with
indicated and matching colors, overcast
edges of A and D-H pieces.
Using brown and embroidery stitches

indicated, embroider detail on A as indicated on graph.

3: With bt. blue, whipstitch B and C pieces wrong sides together as indicated, forming Front assembly; whipstitch Front assembly to right side of A as indicated. Overcast unfinished edges of B and C pieces.

4: With fern, whipstitch E and F pieces to A as indicated. Glue Arms to Sides and Nose, pom-pom and Feet to Back as shown in photo. Glue Holly to Front as shown.

—*Designed by Kristine Loffredo*

A – Back
(42w x 41h-hole piece)
Cut 1 & work.

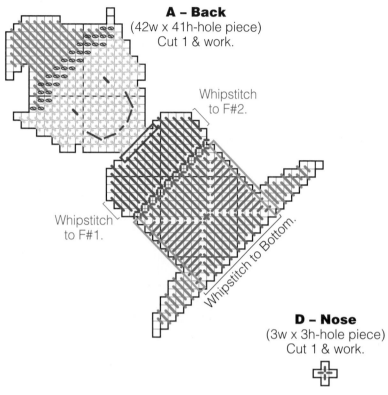

Whipstitch
to F#2.

Whipstitch
to F#1.

Whipstitch to Bottom.

C – Side
(17w x 17h-hole pieces)
Cut 2 & work.

D – Nose
(3w x 3h-hole piece)
Cut 1 & work.

B – Front & Bottom
(18w x 18h-hole pieces)
Cut 2. Work 1 for Front &
leave 1 unworked for Bottom.

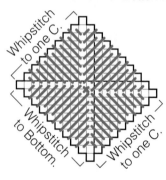

Whipstitch
to one C.

Whipstitch
to Bottom.

Whipstitch
to one C.

F – Arm #1 & #2
(5w x 13h-hole pieces)
Cut 1 each & work.

Whipstitch
to A.

Whipstitch
to A.

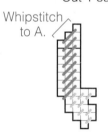

G – Foot #1 & #2
(6w x 13h-hole pieces)
Cut 1 each & work.

H – Holly
(9w x 5h-hole piece)
Cut 1 & work.

Overcast with
Christmas red.

E – Collar
(10w x 10h-hole piece)
Cut 1 & work.

Whipstitch to A.

COLOR KEY: Treat Holder

Worsted-weight		Need-loft®	YARN AMOUNT
	Bt. Blue	#60	11 yds. [10.1m]
	Christmas Red	#02	4 yds. [3.7m]
	Fern	#23	4 yds. [3.7m]
	Flesh Tone	#56	4 yds. [3.7m]
	Christmas Green	#28	1 yd. [0.9m]
	Maple	#13	1 yd. [0.9m]
	Brown	#15	1/4 yd. [0.2m]

OTHER:
- Backstitch/Straight
- Modified Turkey Work
- Collar/Back Attachment
- Front/Back Attachment

Ready, Set, Stitch

Get ready to stitch like a pro with these simple, step-by-step guidelines

Getting Started

Most plastic canvas stitchers love getting their projects organized before they even step out the door in search of supplies. A few moments of careful planning can make the creation of your project even more fun. First of all, prepare your work area. You will need a flat surface for cutting and assembly, and you will need a place to store your materials. Good lighting is essential, and a comfortable chair will make your stitching time even more enjoyable.

Do you plan to make one project, or will you be making several of the same item? A materials list appears at the beginning of each pattern. If you plan to make several of the same item, multiply your materials accordingly. Your shopping list is ready.

Choosing Canvas

Most projects can be made using standard-size sheets canvas. Standard size sheets of 7-mesh (7 holes per inch) are always 70 x 90 holes and are about 10½" x 13½" [26.7cm x 34.3cm]. For larger projects, 7-mesh canvas also comes in 12" x 18" [30.5cm x 45.7cm], which is always 80 x 120 holes and 13½" x 22½" [34.3cm x 57.2cm], which is always 90 x 150 holes. Other shapes are available in 7-mesh, including circles, diamonds, purse forms and ovals.

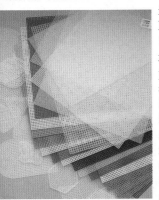

10-mesh canvas (10 holes per inch) comes only in standard-size sheets, which vary slightly depending on brand. They are 10½" x 13½" [26.7cm x 34.3cm], which is always 106 x 136 holes or 11" x 14" [27.9cm 35.6cm], which is always 108 x 138 holes.

5-mesh canvas (5 holes per inch) and 14-mesh (14 holes per inch) sheets are also available.

Some canvas is soft and pliable, while other canvas is stiffer and more rigid. To prevent canvas from cracking during or after stitching, you'll want to choose pliable canvas for projects that require shaping, like round baskets with curved handles. For easier shaping, warm canvas pieces with a blow-dry hair dryer to soften; dip in cool water to set. If your project is a box or an item that will stand alone, stiffer canvas is more suitable.

Both 7- and 10-mesh canvas sheets are available in a rainbow of colors. Most designs can be stitched on colored as well as clear canvas. When a pattern does not specify color in the materials list, you can assume clear canvas was used in the photographed model. If you'd like to stitch only a portion of the design, leaving a portion unstitched, use colored canvas to coordinate with yarn colors.

Buy the same brand of canvas for each entire project. Different brands of canvas may differ slightly in the distance between each bar.

Marking and Counting Tools

To avoid wasting canvas, careful cutting of each piece is important. For some pieces with square corners, you might be comfortable cutting the canvas without marking it beforehand. But for pieces with lots of angles and cutouts, you may want to mark your canvas before cutting.

Always count before you mark and cut. To count holes on the graphs, look for the bolder lines showing each ten holes. These ten-count lines begin in the lower left-hand corner of each graph and are on the graph to make counting easier. To count holes on the canvas, you may use your tapestry needle, a toothpick or a plastic hair roller pick. Insert the needle or pick slightly in each hole as you count.

Most stitchers have tried a variety of marking tools and have settled on a favorite, which may be crayon, permanent marker, grease pencil or ball point pen. One of the best marking tools is a fine-point overhead projection marker, available at office supply stores. The ink is dark and easy to see and washes off completely with water. After cutting and before stitching, it's important to remove all marks so they won't stain yarn as you stitch or show through stitches later. Cloth and paper toweling removes grease pencil and crayon marks, as do fabric softener sheets that have already been used in your dryer.

Cutting Tools

You may find it very helpful to have several tools on hand for cutting canvas. When cutting long, straight sections, scissors, craft cutters or kitchen shears are the fastest and easiest to use. For cutting out detailed areas and trimming nubs, you may like using manicure scissors or nail clippers. If you prefer laying your canvas flat when cutting, try a craft knife and cutting surface – self-healing mats designed for sewing and kitchen cutting boards work well.

Stitching Materials

You may choose two-ply nylon plastic canvas yarn or four-ply worsted-weight yarn for stitching on 7-mesh canvas. There are about 42 yards per ounce of plastic canvas yarn and 50 yards per ounce of worsted-weight yarn.

Worsted-weight yarn is widely available and comes in wool, acrylic, cotton and blends. If you decide to use worsted-weight yarn, choose 100% acrylic for best coverage. Select worsted-weight yarn by color instead of the color names or numbers found in the Color Keys. Projects stitched with worsted-weight yarn often "fuzz" after use. "Fuzz" can be removed by shaving it off with a fabric shaver to make your project look new again.

Plastic canvas yarn comes in about 60 colors and is a favorite of many plastic canvas designers. These yarns "wear" well both while stitching and in the finished product. When buying plastic canvas yarn, shop using the color names or numbers found in the Color Keys, or select colors of your choice.

To cover 5-mesh canvas, use a doubled strand of worsted-weight or plastic canvas yarn.

Choose sport-weight yarn or #3 pearl cotton for stitching on 10-mesh canvas. To cover 10-mesh canvas using six-strand embroidery floss, use 12 strands held together. Single and double plies of yarn will also cover 10-mesh and can be used for embroidery or accent stitching worked over needlepoint stitches – simply separate worsted-weight yarn into 2-ply or plastic canvas

yarn into 1-ply. Nylon plastic canvas yarn does ▮ perform as well as knitting worsted when separa▮ and can be frustrating to use, but it is possible. J use short lengths, separate into single plies and tw▮ each ply slightly.

Embroidery floss or #5 pearl cotton can also be us▮ for embroidery, and each covers 14-mesh canvas w▮

Metallic cord is a tightly-woven cord that comes ▮ dozens of glittering colors. Some are solid-co▮ metallics, including gold and silver, and some ha▮ colors interwoven with gold or silver threads. If yc▮ metallic cord has a white core, the core may ▮ removed for super-easy stitching. To do so, cut ▮ length of cord; grasp center core fibers with tweez▮ or fingertips and pull. Core slips out easily. Thou▮ the sparkly look of metallics will add much to yc▮ project, you may substitute contrasting colors of ya▮

Natural and synthetic raffia straw will cover 7-me▮ canvas if flattened before stitching. Use short lengt▮ to prevent splitting, and glue ends to prevent unravelir▮

Cutting Canvas

Follow all Cutting Instructions, Notes and labels abc▮ graphs to cut canvas. Each piece is labeled with a le▮ of the alphabet. Square-sided pieces are cut acco▮ ing to hole count, and some may not have a grap▮

Unlike sewing patterns, graphs are not designed to ▮ used as actual patterns but rather as counting, cutti▮ and stitching guides. Therefore, graphs may not be ac▮ al size. Count the holes on the graph (see Marking ▮ Counting Tools on page 153), mark your canvas ▮ match, then cut. The old carpenters' adage – "Measu▮ twice, cut once" – is good advice. Trim off the nu▮ close to the bar, and trim all corners diagonally.

For large projects, as you cut each piece, it is a go▮ idea to label it with its letter and name. Use stic▮ labels, or fasten scrap paper notes through the canv▮ with a twist tie or a quick stitch with a scrap of ya▮ To stay organized, you many want to store cor▮ sponding pieces together in zip-close bags.

If you want to make several of a favorite design ▮ give as gifts or sell at bazaars, make cutting canv▮ easier and faster by making a master pattern. From c▮ ored canvas, cut out one of each piece required. F▮ duplicates, place the colored canvas on top of cle▮ canvas and cut out. If needed, secure the canvas piec▮ together with paper fasteners, twist ties or yarn. ▮ using this method, you only have to count fro▮ the graphs once.

If you accidentally cut or tear a bar or two on yo▮ canvas, don't worry! Boo-boos can usually be repair▮ in one of several ways: heat the tip of a metal skew▮ and melt the canvas back together; glue torn bars wi▮ a tiny drop of craft glue, super glue or hot glue; ▮ reinforce the torn section with a separate piece of ca▮ vas placed at the back of your work. When reinforci▮ with extra canvas, stitch through both thicknesses.

Supplies

Yarn, canvas, needles, cutters and most other supplies needed to complete the projects in this book are available at craft and needlework stores and through mail order catalogs. Other supplies are available at fabric, hardware and discount stores.

Needles and Other Stitching Tools

Blunt-end tapestry needles are used for stitching plastic canvas. Choose a No. 16 needle for stitching 5- and 7-mesh, a No. 18 for stitching 10-mesh and a No. 24 for stitching 14-mesh canvas. A small pair of embroidery scissors for snipping yarn is handy. Try using needle-nosed jewelry pliers for pulling the needle through several thicknesses of canvas and out of tight spots too small for your hand.

Stitching the Canvas

Stitching Instructions for each section are found after the Cutting Instructions. First, refer to the illustrations of basic stitches found on pages 156-157 to familiarize yourself with the stitches used. Illustrations will be found near the graphs for pieces worked using special stitches. Follow the numbers on the tiny graph beside the illustration to make each stitch – bring your needle up from the back of the work on odd numbers and down through the front of the work on the even numbers.

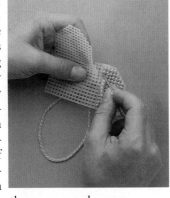

Before beginning, read the Stitching Instructions to get an overview of what you'll be doing. You'll find that some pieces are stitched using colors and stitches indicated on graphs, and for other pieces you will be given a color and stitch to use to cover the entire piece.

Cut yarn lengths between 18" [45.7cm] to 36" [91.4cm]. Thread needle; do not tie a knot in the end. Bring your needle up through the canvas from the back, leaving a short length of yarn on the wrong side of the canvas. As you begin to stitch, work over this short length of yarn. If you are beginning with Continental Stitches, leave a 1" [2.5cm] length, but if you are working longer stitches, leave a longer length.

In order for graph colors to contrast well, graph colors may not match yarn colors. For instance, a light yellow may be selected to represent the metallic cord color gold, or a light blue may represent white yarn.

When following a graph showing several colors, you may want to work all the stitches of one color at the same time. Some stitchers prefer to work with several colors at once by threading each on a separate needle and letting the yarn not being used hang on the wrong side of the work. Either way, remember that strands of yarn run across the wrong side of the work may show through the stitches from the front.

As you stitch, try to maintain an even tension on the yarn. Loose stitches will look uneven, and tight stitches will let the canvas show through. If your yarn twists as you work, you may want to let your needle and yarn hang and untwist occasionally.

When you end a section of stitching or finish a thread, weave the yarn through the back side of your last few stitches, then trim it off.

Construction & Assembly

After all pieces of an item needing assembly are stitched, you will find the order of assembly is listed in the Stitching Instructions and sometimes illustrated in Diagrams found with the graphs. For best results, join pieces in the order written. Refer to the Stitch Key and to the directives near the graphs for precise attachments.

Finishing Tips

To combat glue strings when using a hot glue gun, practice a swirling motion as you work. After placing the drop of glue on your work, lift the gun slightly and swirl to break the stream of glue, as if you were making an ice cream cone. Have a cup of water handy when gluing. For those times that you'll need to touch the glue, first dip your finger into the water just enough to dampen it. This will minimize the glue sticking to your finger, and it will cool and set the glue more quickly.

To attach beads, use a bit more glue to form a cup around the bead. If too much shows after drying, use a craft knife to trim off excess glue.

Scotchguard® or other fabric protectors may be used on your finished projects. However, avoid using a permanent marker if you plan to use a fabric protector, and be sure to remove all other markings before stitching. Fabric protectors can cause markings to bleed, staining yarn.

For More Information

Sometimes even the most experienced needlecrafters can find themselves having trouble following instructions. If you have difficulty completing your project, write to Plastic Canvas Editors, The Needlecraft Shop, 23 Old Pecan Road, Big Sandy, Texas 75755 (903) 636-4000 or (800) 259-4000, needlecraftshop.com.

Stitch Guide

Basic Stitches

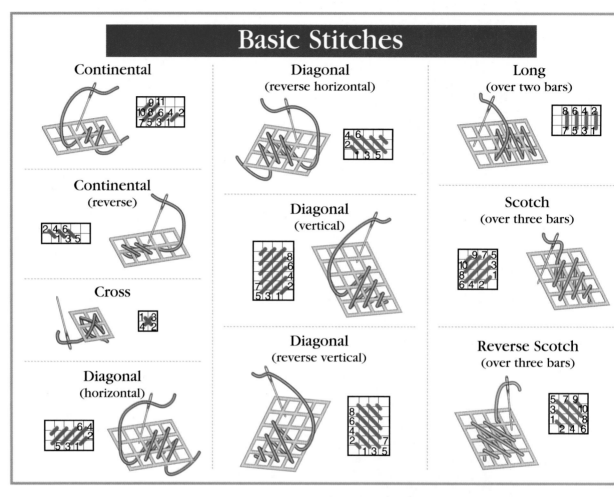

Continental

Continental (reverse)

Cross

Diagonal (horizontal)

Diagonal (reverse horizontal)

Diagonal (vertical)

Diagonal (reverse vertical)

Long (over two bars)

Scotch (over three bars)

Reverse Scotch (over three bars)

Embroidery Stitches

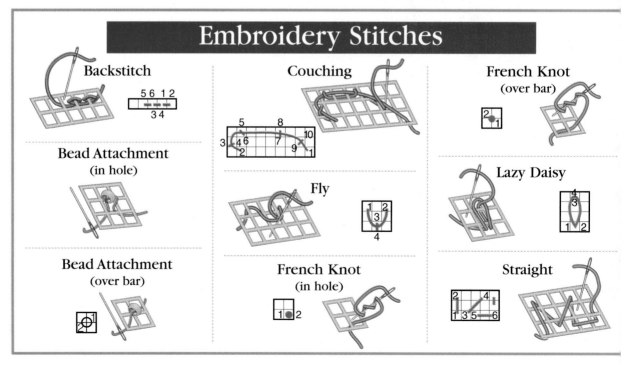

Backstitch

Bead Attachment (in hole)

Bead Attachment (over bar)

Couching

Fly

French Knot (in hole)

French Knot (over bar)

Lazy Daisy

Straight

Specialty Stitches

Alternate Scotch
(over three bars)

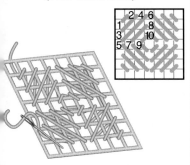

Lark's Head Knot

Lark's Head Knot
(continuous)

Leaf

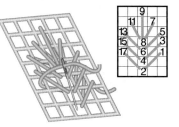

Modified Turkey Work

Mosaic

Sheaf

Shell

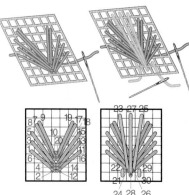

Smyrna Cross

Finishing Stitches

Herringbone Overcast

Herringbone Whipstitch

Overcast

Overcast
(looped)

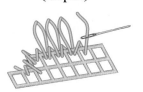

Whipstitch

Whipstitch
(looped)

Acknowledgments

DMC®

Pearl Cotton and Embroidery Floss:
Merry Days, Noel Gift Bags, Nutcracker
Doorstop, Heart Warmer, Card Guard,
Perky Penguin, Winter Welcome,
Elf Door Hanger.

Uniek, Inc.

Canvas and Canvas Shapes: Santa
Bottle Cover, Reindeer Doorstop,
Reindeer Stocking, Reindeer Treat
Holder, Reindeer Frame, Reindeer
Napkin Ring, Quick Baskets, Christmas
House, Ginger People Trivets, Home for
Christmas, Christmas Kitten, Christmas
Joy Blocks, Candy Cane Container,
Holiday Table Runner, Nutcracker
Doorstop, Treat Holder, Stocking,
Napkin Ring, Toy Soldier, Match Holder
Frame, Tote, Soldier Doorstop, Heart
Warmer, Card Guard, Belly Bumpers,
Perky Penguin, Winter Welcome, Elf
Door Hanger, Star Coasters and Bowl,
Elf Stocking, Star Frame, Christmas
Money Tree, Elf Doorstop, Elf Frame,
Elf Napkin Ring, Elf Treat Holder.

Coats and Clark

Plastic Canvas Yarn: Noel Gift Bags.

CPE

Adhesive Felt: Heart Warmer.

Elmore-Pisgah, Inc.

Rayon Crochet Thread: Perky Penguin.

Creative Beginnings

Charms: Toy Soldier.

Beacon Chemical Co.

Fabri-Tac Fabric Glue: Star Coasters and Bowl.

Kunin

Plush Felt: Christmas Ornaments.

Kreinik

Metallic Ribbon and Braid: Reindeer Frame, Reindeer Napkin Ring, Holiday Table Runner, Perky Penguin, Winter Welcome.

Darice®

Plastic Canvas: Pin Weaving Ornaments, Noel Sign.

Nylon Plus Plastic Canvas Yarn: Winter Welcome.

Aleene's®

Designer Tacky Glue: Noel Sign, Winter Welcome.

DecoArt™

Paint: Home for Christmas, Winter Welcome.

Offray

Ribbon: Home for Christmas.

Pattern Index

Antique Lamppost 50
Belly Bumpers 111
Candy Cane Container 68
Card Guard 102
Christmas Candle 48
Christmas House 39
Christmas Joy Blocks 65
Christmas Kitten 59
Christmas Money Tree . . .146
Christmas Ornaments 130
Christmas Place Mat 77
Elf Door Hanger 142
Elf Doorstop 148
Elf Frame 140
Elf Napkin Ring 139
Elf Stocking 128
Elf Treat Holder 151
Frame 92
Ginger People Trivets 46
Heart Warmer 104

Heavenly Trio 54
Holiday Table Runner 71
Holly Accents 63
Home for Christmas 43
Mantel Runner 74
Match Holder 90
Merry Days 6
Music Button Covers 66
Napkin Ring 87
Noel Gift Bags 17
Noel Sign 34
Nutcracker Doorstop 80
Patchwork Stocking 36
Perky Penguin 115
Pin Weaving Ornaments . . .31
Quick Baskets 52
Reindeer Doorstop 14
Reindeer Frame 24
Reindeer Napkin Ring 28
Reindeer Stocking 22

Reindeer Treat Holder 2
Santa Bottle Cover 1
Santa Mask 1
Santa's Snack 1
Snowman Tissue Cover . . .12
Snowman Treat Basket . . .12
Soldier Doorstop 9
Star Coasters and Bowl . . .13
Star Frame 14
St. Nick Tissue Cover . . . . .
Stocking 8
Striped Tissue Cover 7
Tic-Tac Snowman 10
Tissue Cover 9
Tote 9
Toy Soldier 8
Treat Holder 8
Winter Welcome 11

Designer Index

Arickx, Angie 65
Austin, Dawn 46, 111
Britton, Janna 118
Bryce, Ronda 84
Clayton, Candy 59
Dobbs, Phyllis 17
Dorman, Nancy . . .39, 66, 122
Fischer, Kathleen J. 31
Giese, Janelle 115
Hippen, Marlene 77
Laws, Christina 8

Lindeman, Lee 130
Loffredo, Kristine 14, 22,
24, 26, 28, 54, 71, 74, 82, 87, 88,
92, 96, 128, 139, 140, 148, 151
Macor, Alida 36
Maxfield, Sandra Miller . . .10,
            12, 43, 63, 146
Maxfield, Susie Spier 73
McGinnis, Linda 48
Ricioli, Terry 107
Rodgers, Carole 50, 136

Sass, Jocelyn 34
Suber, Kimberly 144
Tabor, Debbie . .19, 52, 99, 124
Vickery, Mike 68, 90
Wilcox, Michele 6, 80, 94,
            102, 104, 142